EASY BEANS

2nd Edition

Fast and delicious
bean, pea and lentil recipes

Trish Ross

BIG BEAN PUBLISHING

Big Bean Publishing
Suite 201-1508 Mariners Walk
Vancouver, British Columbia
Canada V6J 4X9
Email: bigbean@telus.net
www.easybeanscookbook.com

NATIONAL LIBRARY OF CANADA CATALOGUING IN PUBLICATION

Ross, Trish
  Easy Beans: fast and delicious bean, pea and lentil recipes / Patricia
Ross -- 2nd ed.

Includes index.
ISBN 0-9698162-3-5

1. Cookery (Beans). 2. Cookery (Peas). 3. Cookery (Lentils). I. Title.

TX803.B4R68 2003 641.6'565 C2003-903274-4

Cover design, typesetting: Stubblejumper Communications
Text illustrations: Neil Thacker
Cover photograph: Hamid Attie

Printed and bound in Canada
Printed on acid-free paper

Contents

Thanks Everyone

To Moira Chicilo, of Stubblejumper Communications. Without her this second edition of *Easy Beans* would not have become a reality. She is a extraordinary lady who did the cover design, the layout, editing and gave good advice on a range of topics.

To Jean Fremont who did the nutritional analysis, the nutritional chart for legumes and who proofread our information on beans to make sure it was correct.

To Jacquie Trafford, my friend and co-author of the original *Easy Beans* and *More Easy Beans*, who decided that she wanted to move on to another career but whose recipes still appear in the new edition.

To Bob Ross who kept me on track and oversaw our new website.

To family and friends who have been so encouraging and who have eaten more bean dishes then you can imagine and have been honest in their assessment as to whether they should be included in the new book.

To all of you who let us know that you liked the recipes in *Easy Beans* but wanted more nutritional information. We hope this new edition exceeds your expectations.

Why Another Easy Beans?

Since the first edition of *Easy Beans* was published in 1994 and *More Easy Beans* in 1997, there has been increasing emphasis on legumes (beans, peas and lentils) as an important food source. Increasingly, people have been looking for healthy alternatives for the protein in their diets and now look on beans as a mainstream food.

The new edition is the answer to your many requests for more nutritional information. I also wanted to share with you the new recipes that I developed – just can't stop testing and tasting! Included is a nutritional analysis for each recipe and nutritional information about the different varieties of beans, peas and lentils. I am indebted to Jean Fremont, R.D. who analyzed each recipe and provided the nutritional information.

You'll find new recipes for appetizers, soups, salads, main and side dishes. I know you'll enjoy them as much as some of the old standbys.

Thanks for all the positive feedback that we received – it has encouraged me to update and revise *Easy Beans* and bring you the 2nd edition. Enjoy!

NUTRITIONAL ANALYSIS

Registered Dietician Jean Fremont did the nutritional analysis using PC Nutricom Nutritional Analysis Program. The analysis is based on metric weight and measures ingredients in the recipe using:

- the first ingredient where there is a choice
- the smallest quantity of an ingredient where there is a choice
  the smaller number of servings where there is a range (e.g. 4-6 analysis is based on 4)
- garnishes and optional ingredients are not included

Beans are Best

The word is out! Beans are good for you. North Americans have realized what an important food source legumes (beans, peas and lentils) are. There has been an explosion of information about how nutritious they are and the need to include them in our diet.

Two recent food pyramids, the Asian and Mediterranean, developed by the Harvard School of Public Health and the World Health Organization (Cornell University also worked on the Asian Pyramid), have helped legumes gain the recognition they deserve. Both of these pyramids suggest a daily serving of beans.

The Mediterranean Food Pyramid recommends daily servings of grains, LEGUMES, fruit, vegetables, cheese and yogurt. Meat, poultry and fish are served less frequently.

The Asian Pyramid indicates a radical change in a healthy eating program where grains, fruit, LEGUMES and vegetables become the mainstay of any diet and meat and dairy products become optional.

Both the Mediterranean and the Asian Food Diet recommend eating more foods containing plant proteins. Both also encourage more frequent servings of carbohydrates and vegetables. The major difference is that less fat is consumed in the Asian Diet.

Now a new pyramid has been proposed by two researchers from the Harvard School of Public Health (reported in Scientific American,

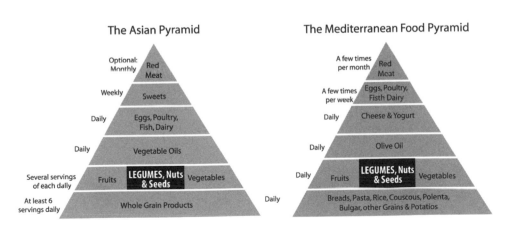

New Food Pyramid

Red Meat & Butter
USE SPARINGLY

Rice, Bread, Potatoes,
Pasta & Sweets
USE SPARINGLY

1 -2 Servings — Dairy

0-2 Servings — Fish, Poultry & Eggs

1-3 Servings — **LEGUMES, Nuts & Seeds**

2-3 Servings — Fruits | Vegetables — In Abundance

At Most Meals — Whole Grain Products | Plant Oils — At Most Meals

Daily exercise and weight control

January 2003). Walter C. Willett and Meir J. Stampfer state, "We have drawn up a new pyramid that better reflects the current understanding of the relation between diet and health. In this pyramid they suggest whole grain food and plant oils at most meals, vegetables and fruits in abundance and one to three servings of nuts and legumes daily. Daily exercise and weight control are also important."

We do not know the exact relationship between diet and disease but it has become accepted that healthy eating can improve our chances of preventing diseases such as heart disease, strokes and some forms of cancer.

LEGUMES provide a healthy food choice because they are:

LOW IN FAT

- The new food guides suggest we choose lower fat foods more often.
- Only about four percent of calories in legumes (except soybeans and chickpeas) come from fat calories.
- Food fats are mixtures of saturated and unsaturated fatty acids. Unsaturated fatty acids, the "good guys", include two types – monounsaturated and polyunsaturated fatty acids. Fats high in monounsaturated fatty acids help to lower blood cholesterol in people with elevated blood cholesterol.

HIGH IN PROTEIN

- The new food pyramids are encouraging us to increase the amount of vegetable protein in our diet.
- Legumes have the highest concentration of vegetable protein of any food.
- The vegetable protein in beans is not complete, but when beans are combined with grains, seeds or nuts they make a complete protein.
- Beans, combined with grains, are a prime source of protein in many countries and have been for centuries.
- Research is showing that plant protein helps protect the heart by lowering blood cholesterol levels in many people.

HIGH IN FIBER

- There are two kinds of fiber: soluble and insoluble fiber
- Legumes are a good source of both soluble and insoluble fiber
- One serving of legumes per day can provide a large proportion of the recommended daily fiber intake (11.5 grams per 1000 calories or about 23 grams for 2000 calories)
- An effective way to add fiber to the diet while cutting fat is to substitute plant sources of protein such as legumes for animal sources like meats.
- Dietary fiber help to enhance the health of the large intestine
- Beans provide lots of fiber which reduces LDL (the bad cholesterol) which can help to combat heart disease.
- Insoluble fiber, once called roughage, helps improve regularity.

LOADED WITH COMPLEX CARBOHYDRATES

- Starch and fiber are complex carbohydrates. Dietary recommendations suggest that carbohydrates supply more than half (55 to 60 percent) of the daily energy requirement. Most of this should be from complex carbohydrates with only 10 percent from simple sugars.
- The Dietary Guidelines for Americans encourage people to choose a variety of whole grain, vegetables, fruits and LEGUMES as good sources of complex carbohydrates.

RICH IN MINERALS AND VITAMINS

- Minerals:
  - high in potassium
  - a good source of iron, magnesium and phosphorus
  - a source of zinc and calcium
- Vitamins:
  - an excellent source of folic acid (folate)
  - folic acid is important for pregnant women to help prevent neural birth defects such as spina bifida
  - folic acid may also have benefits in preventing heart disease

OTHER BEAN BENEFITS

- Gluten free - a good way to add variety to gluten free diets.
- Good for diabetics - both complex carbohydrates and fibre help keep blood sugar on an even keel.

See the chart on the next page for the nutritional analysis of the more familiar legumes.

NUTRITIONAL INFORMATION
for 1 cup/250 mL of canned beans, drained and rinsed

Nutrient	Unit	Navy Beans	Red Kidney Beans	White Kidney Beans	Chickpea (Garbanzo)	Black (Turtle) Beans	Adzuki Beans	Black-eyed Peas	Pinto Beans	Lentils	Lima Beans	Great Northern Beans	Split Peas
Calories		258	223	228	232	244	299	197	238	233	212	303	235
Protein	grams	15.8	15.2	15.6	12.6	16.4	17.5	13.1	14.2	18.1	11.7	19.6	16.6
Fat	grams	1.0	0.9	0.9	3.7	1.0	0.23	0.9	0.9	0.8	0.5	1.0	0.8
Carbohydrate	grams	47.9	40.1	41.0	38.0	43.8	57.8	35.2	44.5	40.5	40.8	55.9	42
Dietary Fiber	grams	10.9	10.6	10.7	8.5	11.1	no data	16.3	9.9	8.0	8.6	14.4	6.0
Calcium	mg	127	49	50	69	50	65	41	83	38.2	56.7	141	27.9
Iron	mg	4.5	5.2	5.3	4.1	2.57	4.7	4.3	4.5	6.7	4.2	4.2	2.57
Magnesium	mg	107	79	81	68	129	121	90	95	72.3	128	136	71.7
Phosphorus	mg	286	250	255	238	259	392	264	278	362	225	361	197
Potassium	mg	670	708	724	412	656	1240	471	812	741	983	933	721
Zinc	mg	1.9	1.9	1.9	2.2	2.7	4.1	2.2	1.9	2.6	1.4	1.7	1.99
Cholesterol	mg	0	0	0	0	0	0	0	0	0	0	0	0
Saturated Fatty Acids	grams	0.3	0.13	0.13	0.38	0.26	0.08	0.23	0.19	0.11	0.13	0.32	0.11
Monounsaturated Fatty Acids	grams	0.1	0.07	0.07	0.83	0.09	no data	0.07	0.18	0.13	0.03	0.05	0.16
Polyunsaturated Fatty Acids	grams	0.5	0.48	0.49	1.64	0.43	no data	0.38	0.33	0.35	0.27	0.43	0.33

Chart compiled by J. Fremont, R.D.

Discovering Bean Varieties

From white beans to yellow split peas, there are a wide variety of legumes used as a food staple in different cultures around the globe. This is not an inclusive list of legumes, but it includes all the beans, peas and lentils used throughout the book.

WHITE BEANS

Navy – a small, white, oval bean. A staple in North American pantries for years. Extremely versatile, from the classic Boston Baked Beans to upscale salads.

Great Northern – the bigger brother of the Navy bean but slightly larger and whiter. It is interchangeable with the Navy bean.

White Kidney – same shape as the familiar red kidney, only white. It is a common substitute in Italian recipes when cannellini beans are called for.

RED BEANS

Red Kidney – as familiar as the navy, especially canned. This bean is dark red and kidney-shaped as the name suggests. Commonly used for chili, but now appearing in salads and soups.

Small Red or Mexican – often called by either name. It is smaller than the kidney, a richer red and has an oval shape. Because of its size, it is a less dominant substitute for the kidney and pinto bean.

Pinto – a pinkish brown, speckled bean traditionally a staple of Hispanic cooking. Now widely used because it combines so tastily with a variety of seasonings. Use in place of red kidney or small red Mexican beans.

BLACK BEANS

Black or Turtle Beans - black, small, oval beans with a glossy coat. Adaptable for every aspect of cooking. (Special note: fermented black beans are black soy beans and have no relation to these beans)

...AND THERE'S MORE

Black-Eyed Peas – cream colored bean with a black spot in the middle. A favorite in southern U.S. cooking; they do not have to be soaked.

Chick Peas or Garbanzo – the same bean with an interchangeable name. Looks like a tan, rough skinned nut. It has an irregular round shape.

Lima Beans – canned and frozen, they are a lovely soft green color. In the dried form, they come in two sizes and are white. The texture is mealy.

LENTILS AND SPLIT PEAS

Green/Brown – labeled green or brown, they are all the same lentil. Small, flattened discs that have a dusty, rather than glossy, look.

Red – actually more a bright orange. Can be used instead of the green/brown ones. The result is a soup that is slightly lighter in color.

Split Peas – both green and yellow. Instantly recognizable and a national favorite in soup.

BUYING LEGUMES

Dried – in bulk or prepackaged.

Canned – cooked and ready to use. Be sure to drain and rinse well.

Frozen – ready to use, but there is not a wide selection.

Organic beans are available both dried and canned.

WHERE TO FIND THEM

Supermarkets - in the bulk food department
                   - with the other canned vegetables
                   - in the specialty areas (e.g., Mexican, East Indian)

Natural Food Stores - in bulk or canned organic
Health and Bulk Food Stores
Ethnic Shops - e.g., Mexican, Greek, East Indian

USEFUL HINTS

It is almost impossible to tell the age of dry beans in the bin unless they are obviously shriveled or cracked. Shop in a popular spot where the turnover is high. Build a rapport with the owner or manager and ask how long the beans have been there. If you try cooking beans that won't soften, take them back and complain. Beans are still suffering the reputation of being difficult to cook simply because the supply was not fresh.

CANNED BEANS & LENTILS

Have every variety in your cupboard for instant meals. Try different brands as some are obviously superior - firm, no burst skins.

Soaking & Cooking Dried Beans

WHAT TO SOAK

Dried beans and whole peas must be soaked before cooking. You do not have to soak split peas, lentils or black-eyed peas. However, they should be rinsed before cooking. There are two soaking methods:

THE QUICK-SOAK METHOD

- Sort through the beans, discarding the broken and shriveled ones.
- Rinse beans under cold running water. A colander is useful for this step.
- Place beans in large saucepan and cover with three times the volume of water (for 1 cup (250 mL) beans, use 3 cups (750 mL) of water).
- Bring to boil. Simmer gently for 2-3 minutes. Remove from heat and let stand for at least one hour.
- Drain beans and rinse under cold running water. Store covered in the refrigerator or freezer if not using immediately.

THE SLOW-SOAK METHOD

- As in the quick soak method, sort and wash beans.
- Place beans in a large bowl. Cover with three times as much fresh cold water as beans (for 1 cup (250 mL) beans, use 3 cups (750mL) of water).
- Let sit for at least four hours or overnight in a cool place.
- Drain and rinse beans. Refrigerate, covered, if not using immediately.

AFTER SOAKING

- If not used immediately, soaked legumes can be stored, covered, in the refrigerator for up to three days.
- Freeze for future use. When frozen, cooked and soaked beans look very much alike. The author must confess to having tossed a salad with soaked beans. You only do it once! Our recommendation is to freeze them after cooking.

COOKING METHOD

- Place the soaked beans in a large saucepan. Cover with at least 3" (7.5 cm) of cold water. Bring to boil. Reduce heat, cover and simmer gently according to chart. Do not boil as skins might burst. Drain and rinse.
- Test for doneness by biting. Try at least five beans from the middle of the pot. They should be tender but firm and don't taste starchy. Do not overcook or you will have "bean mush".
- To prevent foaming, add 1 Tbsp (15 mL) of vegetable oil to the cooking water.

COOKING CHART

Soaked Beans	Cooking Time
Navy	35-40 minutes
Great Northern	40-45 minutes
Pinto	30-35 minutes
Kidney, red or white	35-40 minutes
Black	30-35 minutes
Lima	55-60 minutes
Chick Pea (garbanzo)	80 minutes
Small Red	30-35 minutes
Unsoaked Beans	**Cooking Time**
Black-Eyed Peas	30 minutes
Lentils & Split Peas	20-25 minutes

TIPS

- Add acid foods such as tomato juice, wine or vinegar in the last stages of cooking.
- Microwaves are not a time saver when cooking beans. Handy for heating canned beans and leftovers.
- Cook at least double the amount you need. Freeze the rest for quick use later.

HELPFUL INFORMATION

If your beans aren't tender by the chart times, the reason could be:
- Old beans. Try a more popular market.
- The altitude. The higher you are the longer it takes.
- Hard water. Just keep cooking and "bite" testing.

YIELDS

Most Beans:

1 cup (250 mL) dried = 2 1/4 - 2 1/2 cups (550 -625 mL) cooked

Exception:

Chick peas (garbanzos), lima beans and Great Northern beans yield even more:

1 cup (250 mL) dried = 2 1/2 - 3 cups (625-796 mL) cooked

Lentils:

1 cup (250 mL) dried = 3 cups (750 mL) cooked

Canned Equivalents:

14 oz (398 mL) = 1 1/2 cups (375 mL)

19 oz (540 mL) = 2 1/4 cups (540 mL)

28 oz (796 mL) = 3 - 3 1/4 cups (750- 796 mL)

Exact amounts are not important in bean cooking. Just add a little liquid if the dish looks dry.

STORING

- Dried beans, peas and lentils should be kept in the cupboard in a moisture-proof lidded container. Try to use within six months.
- Soaked or cooked legumes stay fresh for a maximum of three days in the refrigerator. Store in a covered container.
- Freeze beans in portions suitable for the recipes you use. Be sure to label the kind of bean it is as well if it is soaked or cooked.

Bean Companions

We are assuming that your cupboard includes such herbs as basil, oregano and thyme, and spices such as chili powder and paprika. Make sure your dried herbs are not years old. They should be replenished every six months or so. Try buying them in bulk so you can buy smaller quantities. Other bean companions are listed below.

DRIED HERBS & SPICES

- Bay Leaves – a must. Add to beans while simmering. Remove before serving!
- Cajun Seasoning – a large variable blend of peppers and spices. Used in southern cooking.
- Coriander – comes ground or whole. Actually dried cilantro seeds but don't substitute for fresh cilantro – it has a very different taste.
- Cumin (ground) – another must. A spice used in many Mexican and Middle Eastern recipes. Works well with chili powder.
- Curry Powder – a blend of spices common in Indian dishes. Buy a good brand, preferably East Indian.
- Fine Herbs – a combination of basil, thyme, rosemary, dill weed, savory, marjoram and parsley. Great when you can't decide what to use. Get seven for the price of one!
- Italian Seasoning - another combination containing oregano, basil, thyme, rosemary, sage and savory.
- Garlic – fresh is best but when in a hurry you can use garlic powder.
- Garam Masala – a combination of coriander, cumin, cinnamon and cardamon that is used in East Indian cooking.
- Red Pepper Flakes - add fire to any dish. Remember, a little goes a long way.
- Rosemary – works well with white beans and chick peas (garbanzo beans). Combines well with oregano and thyme.
- Savory – called the bean herb because it mates happily with all of them. Add to the beans while simmering.

- Turmeric – an inexpensive substitute for saffron. It gives a pungent taste and a yellow color to dishes.

FRESH HERBS

Use fresh herbs whenever possible. Look for them in the specialty area of the vegetable department. Fresh basil, oregano, thyme, dill weed and mint all add extra flavor. In the summer you might try growing your own. In cooking, the rule is use three times as much fresh to dried. For example, 3 Tbsp (45 mL) to 1 Tbsp (15 mL) dried.

OTHER FRIENDS ARE...

- Cheeses – many cheeses such as feta, Monterey Jack and cheddar combine well with beans. In the exotic category are asiago and gorgonzola. These Italian cheeses are expensive but delicious. A little goes a long way.
- Chilies – we use small canned diced green chilies for convenience. Often called for in Southwestern and Mexican recipes.
- Chipotle Peppers - are jalapeno peppers ripened and smoked. They are extremely hot. Usually canned in adobo sauce (a tomato sauce). Found in the Mexican section of your supermarket or in specialty food stores.
- Dijon Mustard – this French mustard has won us over.
- Grains – bulgar and couscous are used in Middle Eastern cooking and available prepackaged in the specialty section of supermarkets. Also can be purchased in bulk.
- Hot Pepper Sauce – Tabasco sauce is the most common brand and may be used in place of jalapeno peppers.
- Jalapeno Peppers – buy fresh from the specialty area of vegetable departments. Watch out – they can be hot! Use gloves when chopping and discarding seeds. You can also find them canned.
- Olive Oil - choose a good quality extra virgin olive oil; you will notice the difference, especially in salads.
- Salsa – a spicy tomato dip or sauce used to enliven some Mexican recipes. There are a variety of salsas that include chipotle salsa.

- Soy Sauce – used in Oriental cooking. Now available in 'lite' varieties with reduced salt.
- Stock – (vegetable, chicken or beef). If you don't have time to make your own stock (recipe page 61), use good quality bouillon cubes or instant granules.
- Vegetable Oil – Canola, sunflower or safflower are good choices.
- Grapeseed Oil - watch for this one – it's new!
- Vinegars – balsamic, red wine, white wine, cider vinegars, all complement beans. They keep well so stock up.

Clearing the Air

"Well, I'd really like to start including beans in my diet, but..." This is a comment sometimes heard when talking to potential bean enthusiasts. Here are some suggestions to bridge any bean-eating barrier you might have.

But first, what exactly is going on with legumes and our digestive systems? Simply put, the reason for gas after eating beans (and cabbage, broccoli and some fruits) is this:

– complex sugars are not broken down in the upper intestine.

– these sugars pass intact into the lower intestine where they are metabolized (broken down) into simple sugars by bacteria. The byproduct is perfectly normal gas.

To smooth the digestive process, bean cooks try the following:

- Tolerance – the more beans you eat, the less trouble you will have with them. Slip into the bean world twice a week with recipes that do not have beans as the main ingredient (like Bean & Pasta Salad or Black Beans & Rice))

- Preparation – proper cooking is important. After soaking the beans, discard the water and rinse well. Cook in fresh water, discard that water and rinse again. Test at least five cooked beans to make sure there is no starch taste left. Always drain and rinse canned beans.

- Ginger – a staple in East Indian cuisine both for the flavor and its digestive help. Again, add fresh or dried at the cooking stage

- Freezing – we're still being told that it helps to freeze the beans after the soak stage. It's worth a try, but just remember to label the container "soaked" and save your teeth a surprise.

- Kombu – a sea vegetable that appears to have properties which help soften beans. Add a 4" strip to the cooking water after the soak stage.

- Epazote – Hispanic cooks recommend the addition of this weed-like herb to the cooking water. It looks like dried cilantro with a tough stalk. Not so easy to find, but ask for it in specialty food stores.

- Beano – a commercial product found mainly in drugstores, health and natural good stores. It is now a tablet to be taken before meals as well as in liquid enzyme form.

Appetizers

Spicy Bean Vegetable Dip

Company is on their way over for a drink before an evening out. You need an appetizer in a flash. This one takes only as long as rooting out the blender or food processor and tossing everything in. If you have cups of red beans, double the recipe – there won't be an leftovers.

1 cup	canned kidney beans, drained and rinsed	250 mL
1	clove garlic, minced	1
1/4 tsp	hot pepper sauce (e.g. Tabasco)	1 mL
1 tsp	Worcestershire sauce	5 mL
1 Tbsp	mayonnaise	15 mL
	juice of 1/2 lemon	
1 tsp	minced chives or chopped green onions	5 mL
	raw vegetables for dipping	

- In food processor or blender, place all ingredients except chives. Blend until smooth.
- Put in serving bowl and sprinkle with chives.
- Serve with assorted raw vegetables (e.g. carrots, celery, peppers, cauliflower, mushrooms).

Four servings.

> Substitute any kind of canned or cooked beans in this recipe. Add chopped cilantro.

Per Serving:
Protein . . . . 4 g
Fat . . . . 1 g
Carbohydrates . . . . 12 g
Calories 71
Dietary Fiber . . . . 5 g

Black Bean Hummus

If you like hummus, expand your repertoire with our Black Bean Hummus. Double the recipe, so you have extra for Brushettas (page 26), Wraps (page 27) or Southern Pizza (page 114). It freezes well, so you can have some ready at a moment's notice for any of these recipes.

2 cups	cooked or canned black beans	500 mL
1/4 cup	tahini*	50 mL
2	cloves garlic, minced	2
1 tsp	ground cumin	5 mL
1/2 tsp	salt	3 mL
3 Tbsp	olive oil	45 mL
3 Tbsp	warm water	45 mL
	juice of one lime	
	juice of one lemon	

Tahini is a sesame seed paste available in most food stores.

- If using dried black beans, soak or cook 3/4 cup (175 mL) of beans according to the directions on pages 15 and 16. Drain and rinse.
- Set aside a few whole beans for garnish.
- Put all the ingredients in a food processor and blend until you have a smooth paste.
- Place in small bowl. Garnish with parsley or cilantro and the few black beans you have saved.
- Serve with warmed pita bread cut into bite-sized pieces.

10 servings.

Per Serving:
Protein . . . . 4 g
Fat . . . . 7 g
Carbohydrates . . . . 12 g
Calories 123
Dietary Fiber . . . . 3 g

Black Bean Bruschettas

Our version of this bite-size Italian treat. For the base of these appetizers, use the Black Bean Hummus on the previous page. This could become your favorite appetizer as you'll garner rave reviews each time you serve them.

1	baguette, cut in ½" (1 cm) slices	1
1 cup	Black Bean Hummus (recipe page 25)	250 mL
½ cup	grated parmesan cheese	125 mL
Tomato Mixture:		
2	medium tomatoes, minced	2
½ cup	green onions, minced	125 mL
1 Tbsp	olive oil	15 mL
3 Tbsp	fresh basil, minced	45 mL
	freshly ground pepper	

- Place baguette slices on a cookie sheet. Bake in 400°F (200°C) oven, turning once until lightly browned on both sides.
- Spread Black Bean Hummus on top of slices.
- Stir tomato mixture together and spoon onto slices. Top with parmesan cheese.
- Place baguettes on cookie sheet. Bake in 400°F (200°C) oven for 4 minutes or until cheese starts to melt and topping is thoroughly heated.

Yields approximately 30.

Per Piece:	
Protein	2 g
Fat	2 g
Carbohydrates	8 g
Calories	56
Dietary Fiber	1 g

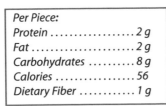

Appetizer Wraps

If you want to wow your friends, but not spend much time in the kitchen, try these easily made appetizers. Make them far enough in advance so that the wrap can be refrigerated for at least an hour.

6	10 inch (25 cm) spinach tortillas	6
1 cup	Black Bean Hummus (see page 25)	250 mL
1 cup	feta cheese, crumbled	250 mL
2	medium red peppers, roasted *	2
	basil or spinach leaves	

To roast peppers: core and seed peppers. Cut in quarters. Place pepper pieces, skin side up on a baking sheet. Bake in oven at 500°F (260°C) for 15 to 20 minutes. Place in paper or plastic bag. Seal and let stand for 15 minutes. Peel off blackened skins.

- Spread tortilla with Black Bean Hummus. Cover with feta cheese, roasted red pepper, cut into strips and a layer of basil.
- Starting at one edge, tightly roll up the tortilla. Cover in plastic wrap and put in fridge for at least one hour (may need to use toothpicks to keep it tightly rolled).
- Cut into one inch (2.5 cm) slices and arrange on a plate with basil leaves as a garnish.

Makes 48 pieces.

Per Piece:
Protein . . . . 2 g
Fat . . . . 2 g
Carbohydrates . . . . 5 g
Calories 43
Dietary Fiber . . . . 1 g

Hummus

You might have a craving for a liberal heap of hummus atop a warmed pita slice – but, alas, no tahini in the fridge. Traditionally, sesame paste is a prime ingredient but this one is made without. Our secret is lots of lemon juice.

2	cloves, garlic, minced	2
1	can (19 oz/540 mL) chick peas (garbanzo beans) drained and rinsed	1
1/3 cup	fresh lemon juice	75 mL
2 Tbsp	olive oil	25 mL
1 tsp	ground cumin	5 mL
2 Tbsp	warm water	25 mL
3 drops	hot pepper sauce (eg. Tabasco)	3 drops
1 Tbsp	cilantro	15 mL

- Combine all ingredients in a food processor or blender. Blend until smooth.
- Present in a glass or pottery bowl garnished with a cilantro sprig.
- Serve with warm pita bread or raw vegetables.

10 servings.

Per Serving:	
Protein	4 g
Fat	3 g
Carbohydrates	12 g
Calories	88
Dietary Fiber	2 g

Santa Fe Bean Salsa

Nothing seems to be more popular today than Mexican cuisine. Enjoy this wonderful variation on the classic salsa and try to stop yourself from shouting, olé! Have cooked or canned black beans on hand for quick preparation.

2 cups	cooked black beans	500mL
1	yellow pepper, chopped	1
½ cup	sweet white onion, chopped	125 mL
1	medium tomato, chopped	1
1	avocado, chopped, optional	1
½ cup	fresh cilantro, chopped	125 mL
3 Tbsp	olive oil	45 mL
	juice of one lemon	
2	cloves garlic, mined	2
⅛ tsp	red pepper flakes	0.5 mL

- If using dried beans, soak and cook ¾ cup (175 mL) of dried beans according to directions on pages 15 and 16. Rinse, drain and cool.
- Combine black beans, chopped pepper, onion, tomato, avocado and cilantro.
- In separate bowl, combine olive oil, lemon juice, garlic and pepper flakes. Add to bean mixture.
- Stir and let stand for at least one hour.
- Serve with taco chips.

12 servings.

Per Serving:
Protein . . . . 2 g
Fat . . . . 4 g
Carbohydrates . . . . 6 g
Calories 62
Dietary Fiber . . . . 2 g

Hot Bean Taco Dip

As many times as this dish has been served, it always gets the same rave reviews. Nothing could be simpler to make!

16 oz	light cream cheese	450 g
8 oz	light sour cream	225 g
1 cup	refried beans*	250 mL
1 pkg	(1.5 oz/39 g) taco seasoning mix	1 pkg
1¼ cups	cheese**	300 mL
	taco chips for dipping	

* Can use canned or recipe on page 138.
** Use a combination of cheddar and Monterey Jack.

- Mix all the ingredients together, except the cheese and taco chips. Blend until smooth. Place in a pottery casserole dish.
- Grate cheese and spread on top of bean mixture.
- Heat at 375°F (190°C) for 20-30 minutes until mixture is hot and the cheese is melted.

Serves 8-10.

> If using canned refried beans look for the "light" variety

Per Serving:	
Protein	13 g
Fat	14 g
Carbohydrates	12 g
Calories	297
Dietary Fiber	5 g

Tapenade

A tapenade is a French appetizer made of green or black olives. At every open air market in Southern France you can buy one of these rich and tasty mixtures. We loved the taste but found it almost too rich so we added chick peas. Our tasters gave this a ten. Makes lots and freeze the extra for the Tapenade Baguette (page 32). Check your deli or specialty section in your store for pitted green olives.

1½ cups	pitted green olives	375mL
1	can (14 oz/398 ml) chick peas, drained and rinsed	1
½ cup	sun dried tomatoes	125 mL
3	cloves garlic, minced	3
2 Tbsp	lemon juice	25 mL
¼ cup	olive oil	50 mL
¼ cup	fresh chopped basil	50mL
½ tsp	grated lemon rind	3 mL

- Combine all ingredients in a food processor and blend until fairly smooth but still slightly chunky.
- Put in a small bowl, top with a couple of sliced olives, and serve with slices of a mini-baguette.

32 servings.

Per Serving 1 Tbsp (18 g):
Protein . . . . 1 g
Fat . . . . 3 g
Carbohydrates . . . . 3 g
Calories . . . . 38 g
Dietary Fiber . . . . 1 g

Tapenade Baguette

If you have some tapenade on hand or in your freezer, try this visually attractive and delicious starter.

1	baguette (not more than 2" in circumference)	1
³/₄ cup	Tapenade (see page 31)	175mL
1	large roasted red pepper, cut in strips*	1
6 oz	soft goat cheese	180 g

*To roast peppers, see directions on page 27.

- Cut baguette in half lengthwise but not quite through. Partially hollow out baguette.
- In hollowed-out halves put tapenade, and on one half cover with strips of red pepper and crumbled goat cheese.
- Press the two halves of the baguette firmly together.
- Wrap in plastic wrap and place in fridge for at least ¹/₂ hour.
- Cut in ¹/₂ inch (1 cm) slices and serve.

Makes 25 pieces.

Per Piece:
Protein . . . . 3 g
Fat . . . . 5 g
Carbohydrates . . . . 10 g
Calories 96
Dietary Fiber . . . . 1 g

Stuffed Mushroom Caps

Your guests will be guessing as they reach for their third and fourth mushroom morsel. What exactly makes them so yummy? Why beans, of course. Much less expensive than the more traditional ham or shrimp filling. This mixture can be made the day before, stored in the fridge and the caps stuffed either in the morning or just before the party.

30	mushroom caps, stems removed	30
1	small onion, chopped	1
1	clove garlic, minced	1
	stems of 15 mushrooms, finely chopped	
1 Tbsp	olive oil	15 mL
1 tsp	dried basil	5 mL
1 tsp	ground cumin	5 mL
1/4 cup	fresh parsley, finely chopped	50 mL
	juice of one lemon	
1	can (19 oz/540 mL) chick peas (garbanzo beans), drained and rinsed	1
1/2 cup	sesame seeds, toasted *	125 mL
3/4 cup	cheddar cheese (medium or sharp), grated	175 mL

To toast sesame seeds, put on baking sheet and bake for 5-10 minutes at 275°F (140°C). Watch them so they don't get too brown.

- In skillet, sauté onion, garlic and mushroom stems in oil over medium heat until tender, about 5 minutes.
- In food processor, combine all the ingredients except mushroom caps and cheese. Blend until smooth.
- Stir in half the grated cheese. Stuff mushroom caps with bean and cheese mixture. Top with remaining cheese.
- Place on baking sheet and bake for 10 minutes at 350°F (180°C). Serve hot.

Makes 30 appetizers.

For each appetizer:
Protein . . . . 3 g
Fat . . . . 3 g
Carbohydrates . . . . 6 g
Calories 57
Dietary Fiber . . . . 1 g

Soups

Classic Black Bean Soup

There seems as many variations of the traditional black bean soup as there are Elvis impersonators! This is the one black bean soup recipe we have found to be "the King".

2 cups	dried black beans	500mL
1	meaty ham bone or ham hock	1
3 Tbsp	vegetable oil	45 mL
2	large onions, chopped	2
1	green pepper, chopped	1
4	cloves garlic, minced	4
10 cups	beef stock*	2.5 L
4	bay leaves	4
1/2 tsp	savory	3 mL
2 tsp	ground cumin	10 mL
1 tsp	dried oregano	5 mL
1/4 tsp	crushed red pepper	1 mL
1/2 cup	sherry	125 mL
	juice of 1/2 lemon	
	salt and pepper to taste	

Can use bouillon cubes or instant beef granules. Follow package directions.

- Soak beans by quick-soak method on page 15. Rinse and drain.
- In large soup pot, sauté onions, green pepper and garlic in oil over medium heat for 5 minutes.
- Add beans, stock, ham bone, bay leaves and savory. Simmer 1 1/2 hours.
- Remove bay leaves and ham hock. Take all the meat from the bone, dice and return to pot.
- Take 4 cups (1 L) of beans and liquid and purée in a blender or food processor until smooth. Return mixture to soup pot.
- Add cumin, oregano, crushed red pepper, sherry and lemon juice. Salt and pepper to taste. Stir well. Heat until piping hot.

Per Serving:
Protein . . . . 16 g
Fat . . . . 7 g
Carbohydrates . . . . 37 g
Calories 285
Dietary Fiber . . . . 21 g

Serves 8.

Puréed Black Bean Soup

Just as fast to prepare as the creamy white bean soup (page 41), as long as you stock cans of black beans in the cupboard.

1	large onion, chopped	1
2	cloves garlic, minced	2
1 Tbsp	vegetable oil	15 mL
2 cups	vegetable or chicken stock	500 mL
2	cans (14 oz/398 mL) black beans, drained and rinsed or 3 cups (750mL) cooked beans	
1 tsp	cumin	5 mL
	springs of fresh cilantro or parsley (optional)	

* Can use bouillon cubes or instant beef granules. Follow package directions.

- If you are starting with dried beans, soak and cook 1^1/$_3$ cups (325 mL) according to directions on pages 15 and 16.
- In a skillet, sauté onion and garlic in oil until brown and beginning to stick to the pan. Add ^{1}/$_4$ cup (50 mL) chicken stock and scrape browned bits free.
- Pour into blender or food processor and add drained beans.
- As the mixture whirls, slowly add the rest of the chicken stock and cumin. Pour into saucepan. Heat gently until simmering.
- Serve in bowls topped with sprigs of parsley or cilantro.

Makes 4 small servings.

If you want to impress your friends or family, this soup presentation will do it. Cut a baguette into ^{1}/$_2$ in (1 cm) slices. Brush both sides of slices with olive oil. Brown in 325°F (160°C) oven for 25 minutes. To serve, put a baguette slice in the bottom of each soup bowl and pour the soup over it.

Per Serving:
Protein .... 15 g
Fat .... 5 g
Carbohydrates .... 35 g
Calories 239
Dietary Fiber .... 8 g

Tomato & Black Bean Soup

A very attractive looking soup with a combination of black beans, red tomatoes and white pasta. Tasty without the ingredients taking time to get to know each other, as is the way with most soups. You could also call this Half-Hour Soup because that's the length of time from first onion chopped to the table.

1	red onion, chopped	1
2	cloves garlic, minced	2
1 Tbsp	vegetable oil	15 mL
1	can (14oz/398ml) black beans, rinsed and drained or 1$1/2$ cups cooked beans	1
4 cups	vegetable or chicken stock	1L
2	tomatoes, chopped	2
$1/2$	red pepper, cut in thin short strips	$1/2$
1 cup	cooked macaroni	250 mL
$1/2$ tsp	freshly ground pepper	3 mL
$1/2$ cup	red wine	125 mL

* Can use bouillon cubes or instant granules. Follow package directions.

- If using dried beans, soak and cook $2/3$ cup (150 mL) according to soaking and cooking instructions on page 15 and 16.
- In soup pot, sauté onion and garlic in oil over medium heat for 5 minutes or until tender.
- Add rest of ingredients and simmer gently for 15 minutes.

Serves 4.

Per Serving:
Protein . . . . 9 g
Fat . . . . 4 g
Carbohydrates . . . . 34 g
Calories 224
Dietary Fiber . . . . 6 g

Picanté Black Bean Soup

We love black bean soup so much we've given you several recipes to choose from. Travel anywhere and you will discover that this type of soup is on most menus. We think black beans are as comforting as turning the electric blanket up to 9.

1	large onion, chopped	1
3	cloves garlic, minced	3
5	strips bacon, cut in narrow pieces*	5
2	cans (14 oz/398 mL) black beans, drained and rinsed or 3 cups (750 mL) cooked beans	2
3 cups	chicken stock**	750 mL
1	red, green or yellow pepper, finely chopped	1
3/4 cup	salsa, medium strength	175 mL
1 1/2 tsp	ground cumin	8 mL

* Kitchen shears cut bacon easily.
** Can use bouillon cubes or instant granules. Follow package directions.

- If using dried bans, soak and cook 1¹/₃ cup (325 mL) according to soaking and cooking instructions on page 15 and 16.
- In a large saucepan, sauté onion, garlic and bacon pieces for 5-8 minutes. Drain the fat.
- Place 1 can or ¹/₂ the amount of cooked beans with 1 cup (250 mL) of chicken broth in a blender or food processor and blend until smooth.
- Add puréed mixture and remaining ingredients to saucepan. Simmer for 30 minutes over low heat.

Serves 4.

Per Serving:	
Protein	16 g
Fat	5 g
Carbohydrates	40 g
Calories	250
Dietary Fiber	10 g

Autumn Vegetable Soup

You'll need a little more time to make this recipe, but it is well worth the effort. Roasting the vegetables really gives this soup a great flavor. This soup can be made all year long but it is especially good in the fall when fresh pumpkin is available. Increase the amount of the other vegetables when pumpkin is not available. Add more seasoning if you like it hotter.

3 Tbsp	olive oil	45 mL
1 tsp	thyme	5 mL
1	butternut squash, cut in 1/2 in (1 cm) cubes	1
1 cup	pumpkin, cut in 1/2 in (1 cm) cubes	250 mL
3	parsnips, cut in 1/2 in (1 cm) cubes	3
3	carrots, cut in 1/2 in (1 cm) cubes	3
2	leeks (white part plus 1/3 of green, chopped)	2
1 1/2 cups	cooked navy beans	375 mL
8 cups	vegetable stock	2 L
2 tsp	chili powder	10 mL
1 tsp	cumin	5 mL

- In a 400°F (200°C) oven, heat oil in 9" x 13" (22 x 30 cm) baking pan.
- Add vegetables and thyme and roast, covered for 20 minutes.
- Stir and roast, uncovered, for another 10 minutes.
- In soup pot, add beans, stock, roasted vegetables and spices.
- Simmer for 20 minutes.

Serves 6 -8.

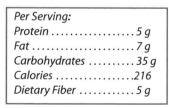

Per Serving:
Protein . . . . *5 g*
Fat . . . . *7 g*
Carbohydrates . . . . *35 g*
Calories *216*
Dietary Fiber . . . . *5 g*

Creamy White Bean Soup

The "not exotic anymore" sun dried tomato is featured in this in-the-door and on-the-table soup. Perfect to take for work lunches in your thermos or a quick heat in the staff microwave. Use any cans of white beans you have in the cupboard. Large jars of sun dried tomatoes packed in oil are readily available and keep for weeks in the fridge.

2	cans (19 oz/540 mL) navy beans	2
	or white kidney beans, drained and rinsed	
2 cups	vegetable or chicken stock*	500 mL
5	sun dried tomatoes (packed in oil), chopped	5
2 tsp	oil (from tomatoes)	10 mL
6	green onions, chopped	6
1/2 cup	sherry	125 mL

Can use bouillon cubes or instant granules. Follow package instructions.

- In a food processor or blender, purée beans and stock.
- In deep skillet, sauté green onions and tomatoes in oil over medium heat until onions are wilted but not brown.
- Add sherry and stir until sherry is reduced by half. Remove from heat.
- Add bean purée to skillet mixture, return to heat and gently stir for 3 minutes.
- Pour into bowls and garnish with parsley or cilantro.

Serves 3-4.

Per Serving:	
Protein	19 g
Fat	4 g
Carbohydrates	56 g
Calories	375
Dietary Fiber	22 g

Minestrone Soup

Another version of an old favorite. Use your food processor to chop the vegetables to cut down on preparation time. Serve it as a hearty supper.

¹/₂ cup	dried navy beans	125 mL
2 Tbsp	olive oil	25 mL
2	medium onions, chopped	2
2	cloves garlic, minced	2
10 cups	water	2.5 L
3	beef bouillon cubes, crumbled	3
3	carrots, chopped	3
2	potatoes, chopped	2
3	stalks celery, chopped	3
2	medium zucchini, chopped	2
1 cup	fresh or frozen green beans, chopped	250 mL
1	can (19 oz/540 mL) crushed tomatoes	1
2 Tbsp	fresh parsley, chopped	25 mL
1 Tbsp	fine herbs*	15 mL
¹/₃ cup	macaroni**	75 mL
	freshly grated parmesan cheese	

*Fine herbs can be found in the spice section of grocery stores.
** Macaroni doesn't freeze or reheat well, so only add it to the soup you're serving.

- Soak beans using quick-soak method on page 15. Drain and rinse.
- In a soup pot, sauté onion and garlic in oil over medium heat for 5 minutes.
- Add beans, water and bouillon cubes. Bring to boil, reduce heat, cover and simmer for one hour.
- Add vegetables, canned tomatoes and herbs. Simmer ¹/₂ hour more until vegetables are tender.
- Add macaroni and simmer for 10-15 minutes or until pasta is cooked.
- Serve in bowls. Sprinkle with freshly grated parmesan cheese.

Serves 10-12.

Per Serving:
Protein . . . . 6 g
Fat . . . . 4 g
Carbohydrates . . . . 23 g
Calories 144
Dietary Fiber . . . . 7 g

Seafood Minestrone

Use whatever white fish happens to be the most reasonably priced at the market. This is another super speedy soup – not the usual major chopping of vegetables as is called for in the typical minestrone recipe. The broccoli gives it a fresh look but other vegetables, such as zucchini, thin-skinned yellow squash or celery could be substituted.

2 cups	cooked navy, great Northern or white kidney beans*	500 mL
1	large onion, chopped	1
2	cloves garlic, minced	2
1 Tbsp	vegetable oil	15 mL
4 cups	chicken stock**	1 L
1	can (28 oz/796 mL) diced tomatoes	1
1 cup	broccoli florets, cut small	250 mL
1 tsp	dried basil	5 mL
1/2 cup	salsa, medium strength	125 mL
1 cup	multicoloured pasta - your choice	250 mL
1 lb	white fish, cut in 1" (2.5 cm) pieces	450 g

* Can substitute 1 can (19 oz/540 mL) of any white bean, drained and rinsed.
** Can use chicken bouillon cubes or instant granules. Follow package instructions.

- If using dried beans, soak and cook 3/4 cup (175 mL) according to instructions on page 15 and 16. Drain and rinse.
- In large saucepan, sauté onion and garlic in oil over medium heat until tender – about 5 minutes.
- Add remaining ingredients except fish. Bring to boil, reduce heat and simmer for 15 minutes.
- Add fish and simmer 7 minutes longer.

Serves 6.

Per Serving:
Protein . . . . 23 g
Fat . . . . 4 g
Carbohydrates . . . . 41 g
Calories 282
Dietary Fiber . . . . 6 g

Jiffy White Bean Soup

This soup is definitely in the category of "through-the-door and on-the-table". It makes a large pot of soup so the recipe can easily be halved (just cut the package of frozen spinach in half and keep in the freezer for another pot of soup). Try a can of mixed beans instead of white kidney beans for variety.

1	large onion, chopped	1
2	cloves garlic, minced	2
2	stalks celery, chopped	2
2 Tbsp	vegetable oil	25 ml
6	medium carrots, chopped	6
7 cups	chicken stock *	1.75 L
1	pkg (10 oz/300 g) frozen chopped spinach	1
2	cans 19 oz/540 mL) white kidney beans, drained and rinsed	2
1 Tbsp	fine herbs **	15 mL

* Can use chicken bouillon cubes or instant granules. Follow package instructions.
** Fine herbs can be found in the spice section of grocery stores.

- In large saucepan, sauté onion, garlic and celery in oil over medium heat for 5 minutes.
- Add stock and carrots. Cook until carrots are just tender. Add spinach and heat until defrosted.
- Add beans, herbs, salt and pepper. Simmer 5 to 10 minutes more.

Serves 8.

Fine Herbs is a combination of basil, thyme, rosemary, dill weed, savory, marjoram and parsley. Great when you can't decide what herb to add!

Per Serving:
Protein . . . . 9 g
Fat . . . . 4 g
Carbohydrates . . . . 29 g
Calories 175
Dietary Fiber . . . . 11 g

Beefy Bean Soup

Although this is speedy to prepare, like many soups its flavor improves as the ingredients get friendlier. A gutsy red wine enhances the taste and adds body.

1 lb	ground beef	450 g
1	large onion, chopped	1
1	clove garlic, minced	1
1 Tbsp	vegetable oil	15 mL
1	small head of cabbage, coarsely chopped	1
1	can (14 oz/398 mL) crushed tomatoes	1
5 cups	water	1.25 L
1 cup	red wine	250 mL
1/4 tsp	crushed red pepper	1 mL
1 1/2 tsp	salt	7 mL
1 tsp	dried oregano	5 mL
1	can (19 oz/540 mL) white kidney beans, drained and rinsed	1
1/2 cup	freshly grated parmesan cheese	125 mL

- In soup pot, cook beef, onions and garlic until beef is well browned.
- With slotted spoon, remove beef mixture. To drippings add oil and cabbage. Cook over medium heat, stirring frequently until tender, about 8 to 10 minutes.
- Add meat mixture, tomatoes, water, wine, crushed red pepper and salt. Bring to boil, reduce heat, cover and simmer for 30 minutes. Add more wine if desired.
- Stir in beans, oregano and parmesan cheese. Heat through, about 10 minutes.
- May serve with additional parmesan cheese sprinkled on top.

Serves 8.

Per Serving:
Protein . . . . 18 g
Fat . . . . 16 g
Carbohydrates . . . . 21 g
Calories 316
Dietary Fiber . . . . 7 g

Chicken Tortellini Soup

Italy meets the Orient in this soup where the problem of leftover chicken or turkey is solved. Serve with crusty French bread.

1 cup	cooked white beans (either navy or Great Northern)	250 mL
½ lb	cheese filled spinach tortellini	225 g
4 cups	chicken broth*	1 L
2 Tbsp	white wine vinegar	25 mL
1 tsp	ground ginger	5 mL
2 Tbsp	soy sauce	25 mL
1 cup	cooked chicken (or turkey), cut in small pieces	250 mL
2	bok choy stems and leaves, chopped	2
3	green onions, chopped	3

Can use chicken bouillon cubes or instant granules. Follow package instructions.

- If starting with dried beans, soak and cook ½ cup (125 mL) according to directions on pages 15 and 16.
- In medium saucepan, heat chicken broth, vinegar, ginger and soy sauce to boiling. Add chicken, beans, onions and bok choy stems. Reserve leaves. Simmer 15 minutes.
- While soup mixture is heating, cook tortellini as package directs. Drain and immediately add to simmering soup. Stir in bok choy leaves and simmer 3 more minutes.

Serves 4.

Per Serving:	
Protein	19 g
Fat	9 g
Carbohydrates	24 g
Calories	255
Dietary Fiber	3 g

Spicy Tomato Soup

This is as warm and soothing as a soup can be – a real comfort food. For sick friends or relatives, it's the "chicken soup" of bean cuisine.

¹/₂ cup	dried navy beans	125 mL
2 Tbsp	vegetable oil	25 mL
1	large onion, chopped	1
2	cloves garlic, minced	2
2	stalks celery, thinly sliced	2
2	cans (28 oz/796 mL) diced tomatoes	2
2	cans 10 oz/284 mL) condensed tomato soup	2
4 cups	chicken or vegetable broth*	1 L
1 Tbsp	fresh parsley, chopped	15 mL
1¹/₂ tsp	dried basil	7 mL
1 tsp	dried oregano	5 mL
1 tsp	dried thyme	5 mL
2 tsp	soy sauce	10 mL
	salt and freshly ground pepper to taste	

* Can use bouillon cubes or instant granules. Follow package instructions.

- Soak beans using quick-soak method on page 15. Drain and rinse.
- In soup pot, sauté onion, garlic and celery in oil over medium heat until tender, about 5 minutes.
- Add tomatoes, tomato soup, broth and navy beans. Bring to boil, reduce heat, cover and simmer for 1 hour.
- Add parsley, herbs and soy sauce. Simmer 5 minutes more. Taste and adjust seasonings.

Serves 8.

Per Serving:	
Protein	6 g
Fat	4 g
Carbohydrates	31 g
Calories	173
Dietary Fiber	8 g

Chick Pea & Coconut Soup

You might call this "a soup for the soul". The combination of curry, lemon grass and coconut milk creates an exotic flavor that is a deliciously soothing meal after a long, hectic day. Lemon grass, often used in Thai cooking, is becoming more readily available at green grocers and Asian markets. If unavailable, you can use 3 Tbsp (45 mL) of dried lemon grass or grated rind/zest of one lemon.

1 Tbsp	vegetable oil	15 mL
1	medium onion, finely chopped	1
2	stalks of celery, finely chopped	2
1	can (19 oz/540 mL) chick peas, drained and rinsed	1
5 cups	vegetable or chicken broth	1.25 L
2½ tsp	curry powder	12 mL
1	stalk lemon grass, outer layer removed and white upper part, chopped finely*	1
1	can (7 oz/196 mL) coconut milk	1
	salt and pepper to taste	

* Cut up the bottom part of the lemon grass stalk and put in soup for flavor.

- In large saucepan, sauté onion and celery in oil over medium heat for five minutes.
- Add chick peas, stock and bottom part of lemon grass stalk and simmer for 15 minutes.
- Remove lemon grass stalk.
- In food processor or blender, purée soup mixture. Return to saucepan.
- Add curry powder and upper part of the lemon grass and simmer 10 minutes more.
- Add coconut milk and heat. Do not let it boil.
- Garnish with parsley or basil.

Serves 4.

```
Per Serving:
Protein . . . . . . . . . . . . . . . . . .12 g
Fat . . . . . . . . . . . . . . . . . . . . . 22 g
Carbohydrates . . . . . . . . . 37 g
Calories . . . . . . . . . . . . . . . . 258
Dietary Fiber . . . . . . . . . . . 7 g
```

Tomato, Garbanzo & Spinach Soup

If Popeye ever gave up his canned spinach in favor of fresh, we're sure his favorite soup recipe would be this one.

1	medium onion, chopped	1
2	cloves garlic, minced	2
1 Tbsp	vegetable oil	15 mL
2 cups	vegetable stock*	500 mL
2	cans (19 oz/540 mL) diced tomatoes	2
1	can 19 oz/540 mL) garbanzo beans (chick peas), drained and rinsed	1
2 tsp	dried sage**	10 mL
3/4 cup	rotini	175 mL
2 cups	fresh spinach, chopped	500 mL
	salt and pepper to taste	

* Can use vegetable bouillon cubes. Follow package instructions.
**6 fresh sage leaves if available.

- In a large saucepan, sauté onion and garlic in oil over medium heat until tender – about 5 minutes.
- Add stock, tomatoes, beans and sage. Simmer, covered, for 10 minutes.
- Add rotini, simmer 10 minutes more. Add more stock if necessary.
- Add spinach and simmer 5 more minutes. Adjust seasonings.

Serves 4-5.

Per Serving:	
Protein	19 g
Fat	8 g
Carbohydrates	87 g
Calories	478
Dietary Fiber	11 g

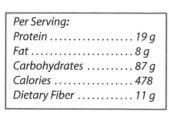

Moroccan Soup

Simmering on the stove, this aromatic soup combines the exotic with the homey feeling always associated with soup "from scratch".

1/2 cup	dried white beans (navy or Great Northern)	125 mL
2 Tbsp	vegetable oil	25 mL
2	medium onions, chopped	2
3	stalks celery, including leaves, chopped	3
1	can (19 oz/540 mL) diced tomatoes	1
3/4 cup	dried green/brown lentils	175 mL
8 cups	water	2 L
2 tsp	ground cinnamon	10 mL
1 1/2 tsp	ground ginger	7 mL
2 tsp	turmeric	10mL
2	saffron threads, crumbled (optional)	2
2 Tbsp	fresh cilantro, finely chopped	25 mL
1/2 cup	fresh parsley, finely chopped	125 mL
	freshly ground pepper	
1	can (19 oz/540 mL) chick peas (garbanzo beans), drained and rinsed	1
	juice of one lemon	
1/2 cup	fine vermicelli, broken into thirds	125 mL

- Soak white beans using quick-soak method page 15. Drain and rinse.
- In soup pot, sauté onions and celery in oil over medium heat for 5 minutes. Add white beans, tomatoes, lentils and water. Bring to boil, cover, reduce heat and simmer for 1 hour.
- Add spices, cilantro, parsley, lemon juice and chick peas and simmer for another 15 minutes.
- Season to taste with salt and pepper. If you want the broth thickened, mash some of the beans against the side of the pot.
- At this point, the soup can be refrigerated or frozen (before vermicelli is added). If using immediately, add vermicelli and cook until tender, about 5 minutes.

Serves 8.

Per Serving:
Protein . . . . 14 g
Fat . . . . 5 g
Carbohydrates . . . . 46 g
Calories 276
Dietary Fiber . . . . 11 g

Quick Mediterranean Soup

This soup earns the Good Housekeeping "double E" award – earthy and easy. It has a satisfying, lingering flavor of turmeric.

1	can (19 oz/540 mL) chick peas	1
	(garbanzo beans), drained and rinsed	
1/2 cup	fresh parsley, chopped	125 mL
1/4 tsp	freshly ground pepper	1 mL
1/2 tsp	turmeric	3 mL
1/2 tsp	ground ginger	3 mL
1 1/4 tsp	ground cumin	6 mL
1	small onion, grated	1
2	medium potatoes, peeled and diced	2
2 Tbsp	tomato paste	25 mL
6 cups	vegetable or chicken stock*	1.5 L
8 drops	hot red pepper sauce (e.g. Tabasco)	8 drops
1/4 cup	lemon juice	50 mL
1/4 cup	fresh cilantro, chopped	50 mL
	salt to taste	

Can use bouillon cubes or instant granules. Follow package directions.

- In soup pot, place all ingredients except lemon juice and cilantro.
- Simmer, covered, until potatoes and onions are cooked, about 30 minutes.
- Add lemon juice and cilantro. Simmer 5 minutes more.
- Adjust seasonings.

Serves 4.

Per Serving:
Protein . . . . 12 g
Fat . . . . 3 g
Carbohydrates . . . . 46 g
Calories 249
Dietary Fiber . . . . 8 g

Leek & Lentil Soup

If your house/condo/apartment is on the market, this is the soup to have simmering on the stove. The wonderful aroma will convince potential buyers that this is the nest for them.

3 Tbsp	vegetable oil	45 mL
2	large leeks (white part plus 1/3 of the green, chopped)	2
1	medium onion, chopped	1
1	clove garlic, minced	1
1 cup	dried green/brown lentils	250 mL
7 cups	vegetable or chicken stock*	1.75 L
2	medium carrots, chopped	2
2	stalks celery, chopped	2
1	can (19 oz/540 mL) diced tomatoes	1
1	bay leaf, crumbled	1
2 tsp	fine herbs	10 mL
1/4 cup	fresh parsley, chopped	50 mL
	salt and freshly ground pepper to taste	

*Can use 7 cups water and 2 large bouillon cubes.

- In a soup pot, sauté leeks, onion and garlic in oil over medium heat until tender, about 5 minutes.
- Wash and drain lentils. Add lentils and stock to soup pot. Bring to boil, reduce heat, cover and simmer for 45 minutes.
- Add carrots, celery, tomatoes, bay leaf, herbs, salt and pepper and simmer for 30 minutes more or until vegetables are tender.
- Add parsley and simmer another 5 minutes. Taste and adjust seasonings.

Serves 10.

Per Serving:
Protein . . . . 3 g
Fat . . . . 4 g
Carbohydrates . . . . 17 g
Calories 115
Dietary Fiber . . . . 3 g

Italian Lentil Soup

Not all wonderful Italian restaurants are in Tuscany. We enjoyed a lentil soup in a superb local restaurant. Too shy to ask for the recipe, we created our own.

1½ cups	dried green/brown lentils, rinsed	375 mL
12 cups	water	3 L
1	small ham hock*	1
2	zucchini, halved lengthwise and sliced	2
2	potatoes, halved lengthwise and sliced	2
2	onions, halved and sliced	2
6	carrots, sliced	6
4	stalks celery, sliced	4
1	can (19 oz/540 mL) crushed tomatoes	1
1 Tbsp	Italian seasoning**	15 mL
½ tsp	salt	3 mL
	freshly ground pepper to taste	

4 beef bouillon cubes may be substituted for the ham hock.
**A blend of 6 herbs found in the spice section.*

- In a soup pot, place lentils, water and ham hock. Bring to a boil, reduce heat, cover and simmer for 1 hour.
- Remove ham hock. Take meat off the bone and dice.
- Add vegetables, tomatoes, herbs and diced meat to lentils. Simmer for 30 minutes more or until vegetables are tender.
- Serve with freshly grated parmesan cheese. Freezes well.

Serves 10.

Italian seasoning is a combination of herbs – oregano, basil, thyme, rosemary, sage and savory.

Per Serving:
Protein . . . . 9 g
Fat . . . . 2 g
Carbohydrates . . . . 17 g
Calories 116
Dietary Fiber . . . . 3 g

Lebanese Lentil Soup

This recipe has been prepared by all our family members for years. Gutsy and good as soon as it's made.

1³/₄ cup	green/brown lentils	425 mL
10 cups	water	2.5 L
4	beef bouillon cubes, crumbled	4
1	medium potato, chopped	1
2	bunches spinach, washed and coarsely chopped	2
2 Tbsp	vegetable oil	25 mL
1	onion, finely chopped	1
3	cloves garlic, minced	3
1 cup	fresh cilantro, chopped	250 mL
¹/₂ tsp	ground pepper	3 mL
2 tsp	ground cumin	10 mL
3 Tbsp	lemon juice	45mL

- Rinse lentils. In soup pot, place lentils, water, bouillon cubes, potato and spinach. Bring to boil, reduce heat, cover and simmer for 45 minutes.
- While lentils are cooking, heat oil in skillet and sauté onion and garlic over medium heat for 5 minutes.
- Add onion mixture to lentils. Stir in cilantro, pepper, cumin and lemon juice. Simmer for 5 minutes.

Serves 6-8.

Cilantro is a fresh herb that goes well with beans. To keep cilantro fresh longer, stand its stems in water in a tall glass and put plastic bag over the leaves. Secure with an elastic. Store in fridge.

Per Serving:
Protein . . . . 7 g
Fat . . . . 4 g
Carbohydrates . . . . 19 g
Calories 135
Dietary Fiber . . . . 4 g

Split Pea Soup

This has been a family favorite for many years. It makes a hearty supper and can be frozen in small containers for an easy lunch.

1	ham hock or leftover ham bone	1
9 cups	water	2.25 L
2 cups	dried split green peas, rinsed	500 mL
1	large onion, chopped	1
2	stalks celery, chopped	2
3	carrots, chopped	3
1 tsp	dried thyme	5 mL
1 tsp	dried oregano	5 mL
1/2 tsp	dried basil	3 mL
1 tsp	sugar	5 mL
	salt and pepper to taste	
1/2 cup	milk, optional	250 mL
	croutons*	

*To make croutons, cut 6 slices of bread (preferably brown) into small cubes. Bake in oven at 250°F (120°C) for about 25 minutes or until lightly toasted.

- In soup pot, combine all ingredients except milk. Bring to boil, reduce heat, cover and simmer for 1 1/2 hours.
- Remove ham hock and take meat off bone. Dice meat.
- If a smooth soup is desired, you may purée all of it in a blender or food processor.
- Return diced ham to soup pot. Add milk just before serving. Adjust seasonings.
- Serve in bowls sprinkled with croutons.

Serves 10.

Per Serving:
Protein . . . . 20 g
Fat . . . . 4 g
Carbohydrates . . . . 42 g
Calories 280
Dietary Fiber . . . . 6 g

Curried Pea Soup

This is definitely a winner – quick to prepare, only one hour to cook and voilà, it is ready to serve! Be sure to use a good quality curry powder.

1 Tbsp	vegetable oil	15 mL
1	medium onion, chopped	1
1	clove garlic, minced	1
1 Tbsp	curry powder (more if desired)	15 mL
1 cup	dried split green peas, rinsed	250 mL
2	stalks celery, sliced	2
2	carrots, sliced	2
1	potato, peeled and diced	1
6 cups	vegetable or chicken stock*	1.5 L
1	bay leaf	1
1 tsp	sugar	5 mL
	salt and pepper to taste	

Can use bouillon cubes or instant granules. Follow package instructions.

- In soup pot, sauté onion and garlic in oil over medium heat for 5 minutes
- Add remaining ingredients. Bring to boil, reduce heat, cover and simmer for one hour or until peas are soft.
- Remove bay leaf and serve.

Serves 6.

Per Serving:
Protein . . . . 9 g
Fat . . . . 3 g
Carbohydrates . . . . 28 g
Calories 168
Dietary Fiber . . . . 4 g

Spicy Split Pea Soup

If you want to try something a little different than the ordinary split pea soup, try this recipe. The chipotle peppers and cumin give a different taste and a bit of a bite.

1 tsp	vegetable oil	5 mL
1	medium onion, chopped	1
2	cloves garlic, minced	2
1 cup	dried green split peas	250 mL
6 cups	vegetable stock	1.5 L
3	carrots, chopped	3
1	can (7 oz/196 mL) tomato sauce	1
1 tsp	canned chipotle peppers in adobo sauce, finely chopped	5 mL
1 tsp	cumin	5 mL

- In large saucepan, sauté onion and garlic in oil over medium heat for 5 minutes.
- Add split green peas and stock. Cook until peas are almost tender, about 20 minutes.
- Add carrots and the rest of the ingredients and simmer until carrots are tender.

Serves 4.

Chipotle peppers are jalapeno peppers ripened and smoked. They are usually canned in adobo sauce (a tomato sauce) and are extremely hot. Look for them in the Mexican section of your supermarket.

Per Serving:
Protein . . . . 14 g
Fat . . . . 2 g
Carbohydrates . . . . 41 g
Calories 227
Dietary Fiber . . . . 7 g

Mulligatawny Soup

This classic eastern soup is not for the faint hearted – the flavors are big and bold. If you like curry, it's "to die for" as one of our favorite friends exclaimed. The lemon juice and soy sauce add an extra "bite".

1 cup	dried split yellow peas, rinsed	250 mL
1 Tbsp	olive oil	15 mL
1	medium onion, chopped	1
1	clove garlic, minced	1
1	medium carrot, chopped	1
2	stalks celery, chopped	2
2 tsp	curry powder (more if desired)	10 mL
1	bay leaf	1
6 cups	vegetable stock*	1.5 L
1/2 cup	cooked rice	125 mL
1	small apple, peeled and grated	1
1 Tbsp	soy sauce	15 mL
1 Tbsp	lemon juice	15 mL
	freshly ground pepper	

Can use bouillon cubes or instant granules. Follow package directions.

- In soup pot, sauté onion, garlic, carrot and celery in oil over medium heat for 5 minutes. Mix in curry powder and sauté for 3 minutes more, stirring frequently.
- Add bay leaf, vegetable stock and split yellow peas. Bring to a boil, reduce heat, cover and simmer for 45 minutes.
- Add rice, apple and thyme. Simmer for 15 minutes more. Remove bay leaf.
- Add lemon juice, soy sauce and pepper. Stir and serve.

Serves 6.

Per Serving:
Protein . . . . 9 g
Fat . . . . 3 g
Carbohydrates . . . . 31 g
Calories 181
Dietary Fiber . . . . 4 g

Two Bean Rotini Soup

If you need a hearty inexpensive soup, this will fill the niche. You can use either the large or small lima beans both of which are readily available packaged and in bulk. The beans you are looking for are white, not green as you might expect.

1 cup	dried lima beans	250 mL
1/2 cup	dried kidney beans	125 mL
6	strips bacon, cut in 1" (2.5 cm) pieces	6
3	cloves garlic, minced	3
3	bay leaves	3
1 cup	celery, chopped	250 mL
1 cup	carrots, chopped	250 mL
1 cup	onions, chopped	250 mL
10 cups	chicken stock*	2.5 L
1 cup	uncooked rotini	250 mL
	salt and pepper to taste	

Can use chicken bouillon cubes or instant granules. Follow package instructions.

- Prepare beans by quick-soak method on page 15. Drain and rinse.
- In a large soup pot, sauté bacon, garlic and vegetables. If bacon does not produce enough fat, add a little oil.
- Add presoaked beans and the rest of the ingredients except the rotini to the soup pot. Simmer, covered, for one hour adding more liquid if necessary. Stir occasionally.
- Add rotini and simmer another 15 minutes, stirring often.
- Before serving, remove bay leaves. Add salt and pepper to taste.

Serves 6-8.

Per Serving:
Protein .... 10 g
Fat .... 14 g
Carbohydrates .... 33 g
Calories 293
Dietary Fiber .... 9 g

Flexible Bean Soup

Three Bean soup, Nine Bean Soup – even 21 Bean Soup – every number of bean soup mixtures is on sale at supermarkets. This is ours and it's called "flexible" because you can use any combination of beans you have on your shelf. A good proportions is 2 to 2¹/₂ cups of dried beans to 10 cups of stock. The lentils and split peas are your thickening agents.

³/₄ cup	each: dried white beans and pinto beans	175 mL
¹/₂ cup	each: dried kidney beans and chick peas	125 mL
2 Tbsp	vegetable oil	25 mL
2	medium onions, chopped	2
3	cloves garlic, minced	3
10 cups	beef or vegetable stock*	2.5 L
¹/₄ cup	each: dried yellow split peas, green split peas and green/brown lentils	50 mL
2	bay leaves	2
1	can (14 oz/398 mL) crushed tomatoes	1
¹/₂	pkg (5 oz/150 g) frozen chopped spinach	¹/₂
1¹/₂ Tbsp	fine herbs**	20 mL
	salt and freshly ground pepper to taste	

*Bouillon cubes or instant granules can be used. Follow package instructions.
**Fine herbs can be found in the spice section of grocery stores.

- Combine beans and soak using the quick method on page 15. Drain and rinse.
- In soup pot, sauté onion and garlic in oil over medium heat for 5 minutes. Add beans and all other ingredients except tomatoes, spinach and fine herbs.
- Reduce heat and simmer for 1¹/₂ hours until beans are tender.
- Add tomatoes, spinach and fine herbs. Simmer for 15 minutes more. Remove bay leaves.
- If you wish to have a smoother soup, remove 4 cups of bean mixture and purée in food processor or blender. Return to pot.

Serves 6.

Per Serving:
Protein . . . . 15 g
Fat . . . . 5 g
Carbohydrates . . . . 35 g
Calories 239
Dietary Fiber . . . . 8 g

Vegetable Stock

When a soup calls for vegetable stock, you can make your own or use good quality bouillon cubes or instant granules to which you add water. Here is a very basic recipe for a homemade stock.

1	large onion, chopped	1
2	large carrots, chopped	2
3	celery stalks, with leaves, chopped	3
8 cups	water	2 L
2	bay leaves	2
1/4 cup	fresh parsley, chopped	50 mL
1 Tbsp	fine herbs	15 mL
1/2 tsp	salt	3 mL
	freshly ground pepper to taste	

- In large soup pot, combine all ingredients. Bring to boil, cover and simmer for 1 hour.
- Strain. Discard vegetables.
- Freezes well.

Makes 7-8 cups.

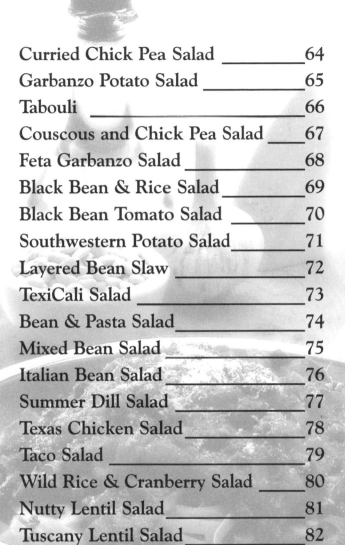

Salads

Curried Chick Pea Salad

It's best to double this recipe because everyone comes back for seconds!
Be sure to use a good curry powder – it makes all the difference.

1	can (14 oz/396 mL) chick peas, drained and rinsed	1
1	pkg (6 oz/170 g) long grain and wild rice	1
1/2 cup	golden raisins, coarsely chopped	125 mL
1/3 cup	dried apricots, coarsely chopped	75 mL
2 Tbsp	toasted almond flakes (optional)	25 mL
Dressing:		
1 1/2 Tbsp	olive oil	20 mL
1 Tbsp	white wine vinegar	15 mL
1 tsp	lemon juice	5 mL
1 tsp	honey	5 mL
2 tsp	curry powder	10 mL

- Cook long grain and wild rice mixture according to package directions.
- In bowl combine rice with all other salad ingredients except almonds.
- In tightly lidded jar, combine dressing ingredients. Shake well and and add to salad ingredients. Toss to coat.
- If desired top with toasted almond flakes.

Serves 4.

Per Serving:
Protein . . . . 8 g
Fat . . . . 5 g
Carbohydrates . . . . 53 g
Calories 276
Dietary Fiber . . . . 5 g

Garbanzo Potato Salad

Easy to expand for a crowd. If your potatoes are mealy (sometimes its hard to tell when you're buying them) they tend to absorb the dressing all too readily. If the salad seems dry, mix up some more dressing and add until you've got the right balance.

3 cups	cooked, peeled and cubed potatoes	750 mL
1 cup	uncooked carrots, sliced thinly	250 mL
1	red onion, sliced thinly	1
1 cup	canned garbanzo beans (chick peas), drained and rinsed	250 mL
Dressing:		
1/2 cup	wine vinegar	125 mL
1/4 cup	vegetable oil	50 mL
1/2 tsp	sugar	3 mL
2	cloves garlic, minced	2
	salt and pepper to taste	

- Steam carrots until just tender – about 4 minutes.
- Place all the salad ingredients together in a large bowl.
- In a tightly lidded jar combine dressing ingredients. Shake well.
- Pour dressing over salad and stir well.
- Chill in fridge for 2 hours.

Serves 4-6.

Per Serving:
Protein . . . . *9 g*
Fat . . . . *13 g*
Carbohydrates . . . . *46 g*
Calories *328*
Dietary Fiber . . . . *5 g*

Tabouli

Tastiest when fresh mint is available. During the winter, dried mint is acceptable or you can leave the mint out together. Bulgar wheat is now universally available in bulk or prepackaged at your local grocery store. The amount of the vegetables can be varied without detriment to the flavor – we lean towards lots of parsley.

1¹/₂ cups	bulgar wheat (cracked wheat)	375 mL
1	can (19 oz/540 mL) chick peas (garbanzo beans), drained and rinsed	1
1¹/₂ cups	fresh parsley, chopped	375 mL
³/₄ cup	fresh mint, chopped	175 mL
³/₄ cup	green onions, chopped	175 mL
³/₄ cup	tomatoes, cut into small pieces	175 mL
Dressing:		
¹/₄ cup	vegetable oil	50 mL
¹/₂ cup	lemon juice	125 mL
	salt and pepper to taste	

- Place bulgar wheat in a bowl and pour boiling water to cover by at least one inch. Let stand for ¹/₂ hour until all the water has been absorbed. Drain any excess and pat dry with a paper towel if necessary.
- Stir in remaining ingredients except dressing.
- In small bowl, whisk oil, lemon juice and salt and pepper. Pour over salad and mix well.
- Chill in fridge for at least one hour. This salad, covered and cold, will keep for up to four days.

Serves 8.

Use fresh herbs when possible. Just remember to use 3 times as much as the dried herb.

Per Serving:
Protein . . . . 9 g
Fat . . . . 7 g
Carbohydrates . . . . 41 g
Calories 257
Dietary Fiber . . . . 5 g

Couscous & Chick Pea Salad

This salad really needs fresh mint to make it perfect. In the summer, there's lots but in the winter it is always a major search in the produce department. Sometimes it's available, sometimes not.

1³/₄ cups	water	425 mL
1 cup	couscous	250 mL
1	can (14 oz/396 mL) chick peas (garbanzo beans), drained and rinsed	1
2	small red peppers, chopped	2
4	green onions, thinly sliced	4
2	medium carrots, finely chopped	2
¹/₂ cup	pitted Greek olives, sliced	125 mL
6 oz.	feta cheese, crumbled	170 g
Dressing:		
6 Tbsp	fresh mint	90 mL
1¹/₂ Tbsp	white wine vinegar	20 mL
1	clove garlic, minced	1
¹/₂ tsp	Dijon mustard	3 mL
¹/₄ tsp	sugar	1 mL
¹/₃ cup	olive oil	75 mL

- In medium sauce pan, bring water to boil. Add couscous.
- Remove from heat, cover and let stand for 5 minutes.
- In large bowl place couscous and fluff with a fork. Add all other salad ingredients except feta cheese.
- In food processor or blender, add all dressing ingredients except oil. Process a few seconds until mint is finely chopped. Gradually add oil and process until well blended.
- Pour dressing over salad. Toss. Add feta cheese and stir gently.
- Arrange lettuce around edge of large platter or glass salad bowl. Mound salad in the center.

Serves 6-8.

Per Serving:
Protein . . . . 14 g
Fat . . . . 24 g
Carbohydrates . . . . 47 g
Calories 451
Dietary Fiber . . . . 5 g

Feta Garbanzo Salad

Shades of the Greek Isles – this salad is easy to whip up for either a simple family supper or a dinner party.

1	can (19 oz/540 mL) garbanzo beans (chick peas), drained and rinsed	1
1/2 cup	black olives, sliced	125 mL
1	red onion, chopped	1
1/2 cup	feta cheese, crumbled	125 mL
1/2 cup	fresh parsley, chopped	125 mL
Dressing:		
1/4 cup	vegetable oil	50 mL
2 Tbsp	lemon juice	25 mL
1/4 tsp	black pepper	1 mL
1/2 tsp	dried oregano	2 mL
1 tsp	Dijon mustard	5 mL

- In medium bowl, mix garbanzo beans, olives, onions, cheese and parsley.
- In tightly lidded jar, combine dressing ingredients. Shake well.
- Pour dressing on salad mixture. Stir.
- Chill in refrigerator for one hour.
- Serve in a lettuce-lined glass or pottery dish.

Serves 4.

To add zest to a tossed salad, spoon any leftover bean salad over lettuce or spinach.

Per Serving:
Protein . . . . 16 g
Fat . . . . 45 g
Carbohydrates . . . . 38 g
Calories 604
Dietary Fiber . . . . 7 g

Black Bean & Rice Salad

This tangy salad is very colorful with its yellow corn, black beans and red pepper pieces. We've heard from many that this recipe is their favorite.

3/4 cup	dried black beans*	175 mL
1 cup	cooked long grain rice	250 mL
1/2 cup	kernel corn, canned or fresh	125 mL
1	sweet red pepper, chopped	1
3	green onions, chopped	3
2 Tbsp	fresh cilantro, chopped	25 mL
2 Tbsp	fresh parsley, chopped	25 mL
Dressing:		
1/4 cup	olive oil	50 mL
2 Tbsp	red wine vinegar	25 mL
1 Tbsp	lemon juice	15 mL
1 1/2 tsp	chili powder (or to taste)	8 mL
1	clove garlic, minced	1
1/2 tsp	ground cumin (or to taste)	3 mL
	salt and pepper to taste	

Can use 1 can (19 oz/540 mL) of black beans, drained and rinsed.

- Quick-soak and cook beans according to instructions on pages 15 and 16 (be sure not to overcook – you want them just tender but not mushy). Rinse and cool.
- In salad bowl, combine all ingredients except dressing.
- Pour over salad and toss gently.
- Refrigerate for several hours before serving. Still good three days later.

Serves 6.

Per Serving:	
Protein	. . . . 7 g
Fat	. . . . 8 gg
Carbohydrates	. . . . 29 g
Calories	 209
Dietary Fiber	. . . . 10 g

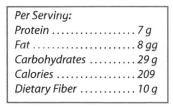

Black Bean Tomato Salad

With the availability of fresh herbs in the supermarket, this salad can be enjoyed all year round. Another one that can be prepared very quickly using leftover or canned beans. This recipe is very eye-appealing served in a glass salad bowl.

4	ripe tomatoes, cut in chunks	4
1¹/₄ cup	feta cheese, cut in chunks, half the size of the tomatoes	300 mL
¹/₃ cup	black beans, cooked or canned	75 mL
¹/₄ cup	fresh basil	50 mL
Dressing:		
3 Tbsp	olive oil	45 mL
2	cloves garlic, minced	2
¹/₂ tsp	sugar	3 mL
¹/₄ tsp	freshly ground pepper	1 mL

- Prepare first four ingredients and place in salad bowl. Stir gently to mix.
- In tightly lidded jar, combine dressing ingredients. Shake well. Pour over salad mixture and toss lightly.
- Let stand for one hour in the refrigerator. Keeps for three days if tomatoes are firm.

Serves 4.

Per Serving:	
Protein	*14 g*
Fat	*28 g*
Carbohydrates	*13 g*
Calories	*351*
Dietary Fiber	*2 g*

Southwestern Potato Salad

If you have been making the same traditional potato salad for more years than you would care to admit, here's a new one. We guarantee instant approval and widespread demand for copies of this recipe! It also uses up those cooked black beans hiding in the freezer.

6	large red or white, thin skinned potatoes	6
1/2 lb	bacon	225 g
1	can (4 oz/114 mL) diced green chilies, drained	1
1/2 cup	cooked black beans	125 mL
1/2 cup	fresh parsley, chopped	125 mL
1/2 cup	red onion, chopped	125 mL
Dressing:		
3 Tbsp	vegetable oil	45 mL
1/3 cup	white wine vinegar	75 mL
1/2 tsp	ground cumin	3 mL
	freshly ground pepper	
1/2 tsp	salt	3 mL

- Cook unpeeled potatoes in covered saucepan for 20 minutes or until just tender. Drain and let cool.
- Cook bacon in skillet until crisp. Remove, pat dry and crumble.
- In large salad bowl, cube unskinned potatoes. Add remaining ingredients.
- In tightly lidded jar, combine dressing ingredients. Shake well. Pour over salad mixture and toss lightly.
- Cover and refrigerate for at least two hours so that the ingredients "get to know each other".

Serves 6.

Per Serving:
Protein . . . . 15 g
Fat . . . . 19 g
Carbohydrates . . . . 30 g
Calories 345
Dietary Fiber . . . . 4 g

Layered Bean Slaw

This recipe can be expanded or contracted depending on the number of people you are feeding. Be experimental with the layers but be sure to show it off in a glass bowl. Why not play the role of maestro and toss it at the table!

1	red onion, cut in rings and halved	1
2 cups	shredded green cabbage	500 mL
2	tomatoes, sliced and halved	2
1	small cucumber, thinly slices	1
1	pepper, yellow, green or red	1
1	can (14 oz/398 mL) black bean, drained and rinsed or 1½ cups cooked*	1
¾ cup	feta cheese, crumbled	175 mL
Dressing:		
½ cup	vegetable oil	125 mL
⅓ cup	red wine vinegar	75 mL
2	cloves garlic, minced	2
½ tsp	ground cumin	3 mL
	salt and pepper to taste	

If using dried beans, soak and cook 3/4 cup (175 mL) according to directions on pages 15 and 16.

- In glass bowl, layer ingredients in the order listed, starting with the onion on the bottom and finishing with a top layer of feta cheese. Cover and refrigerate.
- In tightly lidded jar, combine dressing ingredients. Shake well.
- When ready to serve salad, pour on dressing and take to the table. Toss in front of family or guests.

Serves 6.

Per Serving:
Protein . . . . 10 g
Fat . . . . 26 g
Carbohydrates . . . . 19 g
Calories 345
Dietary Fiber . . . . 5 g

TexiCali Salad

Colorful, tangy, and hearty – a perfect fair-weather meal. Try making it in the fall when vine-picked tomatoes are at their finest.

1	red onion, chopped	1
5	tomatoes, chopped	5
1	small green pepper, chopped	1
1	small red pepper, chopped	1
1	can (19 oz/540 mL) black beans, drained and rinsed	1
1	can (12 oz/341 mL) kernel corn, drained	1
1	head of romaine lettuce	1
1½ cups	grated cheddar cheese	375 mL
2 cups	crushed tortilla chips	500 mL
Dressing:		
⅓ cup	cilantro	75 mL
½ cup	lime juice	125 mL
½ cup	olive oil	125 mL
½ cup	sour cream	125 mL
1 tsp	sugar	5 mL
½ tsp	salt	3 mL
½ tsp	freshly ground pepper	3 mL

- Combine all ingredients except lettuce, cheese and tortilla chips.
- Tear lettuce into bite size pieces and place in glass bowl. Top with bean mixture.
- In blender, combine dressing ingredients and blend.
- Combine dressing with salad ingredients and gently mix. Top with grated cheese and tortilla chips.

Per Serving:
Protein . . . . 18 g
Fat . . . . 36 g
Carbohydrates . . . . 49 g
Calories 573
Dietary Fiber . . . . 7 g

Serves 6.

Bean & Pasta Salad

This very colorful, large salad is perfect for luncheons or to take along on a group picnic. It is easy to assemble if you have cooked beans already prepared and waiting in your freezer. The French dressing used on this salad is excellent with any tossed salad so you may want to make extra and keep it in your fridge.

1 cup	each cooked kidney, black, chick peas (garbanzo beans), and navy beans*	250 mL
2 cups	vegetable rotini, cooked**	500 mL
1	green pepper, chopped	1
1/2 cup	white onion, chopped	125 mL
1/4 cup	fresh parsley, chopped	50 mL
1 Tbsp	fresh basil (1 tsp/5 mL dried)	15 mL
1 Tbsp	fresh thyme (1 tsp/5 mL dried)	15 mL
French Dressing:		
2 Tbsp	white vinegar	25 mL
2 Tbsp	tomato ketchup	25 mL
1 Tbsp	brown sugar	15 mL
1/2 tsp	paprika	3 mL
2 tsp	lemon juice	10 mL
2 tsp	grated onion	10 mL
1/4 cup	oil (combination of half olive oil and half vegetable oil works well)	50 mL

Use any combination of 4 cups leftover cooked or canned beans.
*** If unavailable, use plain rotini.*

- If using canned beans, drain and rinse.
- In large salad bowl, combine beans, rotini, vegetables and herbs.
- In tightly lidded jar, combine all dressing ingredients except oil. Blend well. Add oil and shake well.
- Add dressing to bean mixture. Stir gently. Cover and refrigerate for several hours to meld flavors.

Serves 8-10.

Per Serving:
Protein . . . . 12 g
Fat . . . . 7 g
Carbohydrates . . . . 46 g
Calories 291
Dietary Fiber . . . . 9 g

Mixed Bean Salad

When it rains on your golf holiday in Southern California and you're a bean nut, what would you do? Naturally, you're off to sample the local bean cuisine. These delightful mixed beans were served in small bowls as an appetizer with warmed brown bread.

1 cup	fresh green beans, cut in 1/2" (1 cm) pieces	250 mL
1	can (19 oz/540 mL) chick peas	1
1	can (19 oz/540 mL) kidney beans	1
1	small sweet white onion, chopped	1
2 Tbsp	fresh parsley, chopped	25 mL
Lemon Dressing:		
1/4 cup	lemon juice	50 mL
3 Tbsp	olive oil	45 mL
2 tsp	Dijon mustard (grainy is nice)	10 mL
1 tsp	grated lemon rind (zest)	5 mL
1/2 tsp	freshly ground pepper	3 mL
1 tsp	sugar (optional)	5 mL

- Steam green beans for about 5 minutes until crunchy but not soft.
- Drain and rinse canned beans. Combine beans with onion and parsley.
- In tightly lidded jar, combine dressing ingredients. Shake well.
- Pour over salad and toss gently. Let stand for several hours for best flavor.
- Serve on a bed of lettuce or spooned over a tossed salad.

Serves 4.

Try using pesto sauce as the dressing in any of the mixed bean salads.

Per Serving:
Protein . . . . 18 g
Fat . . . . 14 g
Carbohydrates . . . . 56 g
Calories 408
Dietary Fiber . . . . 16 g

Italian Bean Salad

It's amazing how how quickly you can put this scrumptious salad together. Cans of mixed beans are the secret.

2	cans (19 oz/540 mL) mixed beans, drained and rinsed	2
1/2 cup	finely chopped sun dried tomatoes	125 mL
1/2 cup	canned artichoke hearts, chopped	125 mL
1/4 cup	chopped fresh basil	50 mL
3 Tbsp	chopped pine nuts	45 mL
1/4 cup	sliced black olives (optional)	50 mL
Dressing:		
2 Tbsp	olive oil	25 mL
2 Tbsp	sweet white wine vinegar	25 mL

- In glass salad bowl, mix all salad ingredients except basil and pine nuts.
- In tightly lidded jar, combine dressing ingredients. Shake well.
- Add to salad ingredients. Cover and refrigerate for at least an hour.
- Just before serving add basil and pine nuts.

Serves 6

Per Serving:
Protein . . . . 15 g
Fat . . . . 7 g
Carbohydrates . . . . 42 g
Calories 281
Dietary Fiber . . . . 13 g

Summer Dill Salad

For those dill fans out there, this salad will more than satisfy your craving. Serve this salad in the summer when fresh dill is at its best.

2	cans (19 oz/540 mL) mixed beans, drained and rinsed	2
¹/₂ cup	diced red onion	125 mL
10	fresh dill heads, chopped	10
Dressing:		
2 Tbsp	olive oil	25 mL
2 Tbsp	white wine vinegar	25 mL
1 tsp	Dijon mustard	5 mL
1 tsp	sugar	5 mL

- In salad bowl combine beans with onion and dill.
- In tightly lidded jar, combine dressing ingredients. Shake well.
- Pour over salad and toss.
- Cover and refrigerate for at least one hour.

Serves 4.

Legumes (beans, peas and lentils) have the highest concentration of vegetable protein of any food. The vegetable protein in beans is not complete, but when beans are combined with grains, seeds or nuts they make a complete protein.

Per Serving:
Protein . . . . 16 g
Fat . . . . 7 g
Carbohydrates . . . . 48 g
Calories 309
Dietary Fiber . . . . 19 g

Texas Chicken Salad

A dinner staple for lazy summer days. Leftover roasted or barbecued chicken can be used as well as starting from scratch. Best of all, it can be eaten with a napkin tucked under your chin, lounging in a deck chair.

2	chicken breasts, skinned and cubed	2
2 Tbsp	vegetable oil	25 mL
1/2 cup	salsa, medium strength	125 mL
1/2 cup	light salad dressing or mayonnaise	125 mL
1/2 tsp	hot pepper sauce (e.g. Tabasco)	3 mL
1	avocado, chopped	1
2	medium tomatoes, chopped	2
3 cups	shredded lettuce	750 mL
3 cups	tortilla chips	750 mL
1	can (19 oz/540 mL) red kidney beans, drained and rinsed	1
1/2 cup	Monterey Jack cheese, grated	125 mL

- In skillet, heat oil and stir-fry chicken for 5 minutes or until pink disappears. Stir in salsa and simmer for 5 more minutes.
- Place tomatoes and avocados in a bowl.
- Combine salad dressing and hot pepper sauce. Add to tomatoes and avocados and stir gently.
- On large serving plate or individual plates, layer in the following order: start with chips, then lettuce, beans, chicken and ending with tomato and avocado mixture. Top with cheese.

Serves 6.

Per Serving:
Protein . . . . 28 g
Fat . . . . 24 g
Carbohydrates . . . . 31 g
Calories 443
Dietary Fiber . . . . 6 g

Taco Salad

This is a "complete meal" salad to serve on a hot summer night or when you are having guests for lunch. Everything can be prepared ahead and tossed together at the last moment.

1	large onion, chopped	1
1	clove garlic, minced	1
1 Tbsp	vegetable oil	15 mL
1/2 lb	lean ground beef	225 g
1	can (7 1/2 oz/213 mL) tomato sauce	1
1 tsp	chili powder (more if desired)	5 mL
1 tsp each	ground cumin, dried oregano	5 mL each
	freshly ground pepper to taste	
1	large head iceberg or leaf lettuce	1
2	large tomatoes, chopped	2
1	can (14 oz/398 mL) kidney beans, drained and rinsed	1
1/2 cup	black olives, sliced (optional)	125 mL
1	avocado, chopped (optional)	1
2 cups	taco or corn chips	500 mL
1/2 cup	grated cheddar or Monterey Jack cheese	125 mL
Dressing:		
1/3 cup	vegetable oil	75 mL
3 Tbsp	wine vinegar	45 mL
1/4 tsp each	salt, sugar, dry mustard	1 mL each

- In skillet, sauté onion and garlic in oil over medium heat for about 5 minutes. Add beef and brown. Drain excess fat.
- Add tomato sauce, spices and oregano. Simmer for 10 minutes. Cool.
- Cut lettuce in bite-sized pieces and place in large salad bowl.
- Combine meat mixture, tomatoes, kidney beans, olives, avocado and 1/2 the taco chips. Add to lettuce.
- In tightly lidded jar, combine dressing ingredients. Shake well.
- Combine dressing with salad ingredients. Mix gently. Top with other half of the taco chips and cheese.

Serves 6-8.

```
Per Serving:
Protein .................. 17 g
Fat ...................... 33 g
Carbohydrates .......... 34 g
Calories ................. 489
Dietary Fiber ............ 5 g
```

Wild Rice & Cranberry Salad

A variation of this salad was served at a Charles Dickens dinner. It made a perfect accompaniment to the turkey dinner. After experimenting, we liked this version, so next time you have turkey, do try it. This salad is so delicious, your guests will implore, "please, may I have some more?".

1/2 cup	wild rice	125 mL
3 cups	water	750 mL
1/3 cup	green/brown lentils	75 mL
1	red pepper, thinly sliced and cut in half	1
1	yellow pepper, thinly sliced and cut in half	1
1/2 cup	dried cranberries, coarsely chopped	125 mL
Dressing:		
1 Tbsp	salad oil	15 mL
1 Tbsp	white balsamic vinegar	15 mL
1 Tbsp	orange juice	15 mL
1 tsp	honey	5 mL
1/2 tsp	cumin	3 mL

- Add wild rice to water. Bring to boil and cook covered over medium heat for 30 minutes. Drain.
- While rice is cooking, cover lentils with water and cook for 25 minutes until tender. Drain and rinse (you may use 1 cup (250mL) canned lentils, drained and rinsed).
- In a medium glass bowl, combine rice, lentils, peppers and cranberries.
- In tightly lidded jar, combine dressing ingredients. Shake well.
- Combine dressing with salad ingredients.

Serves 4.

Per Serving:
Protein . . . . 11 g
Fat . . . . 4 g
Carbohydrates . . . . 50 g
Calories 267
Dietary Fiber . . . . 6 g

True balsamic vinegar is made from red grapes, but because of its popularity some makers of sweet white wine vinegar have labeled theirs "white balsamic vinegar"

Nutty Lentil Salad

From humble to fashionable – that's the story of the lentil. Innovative chefs appreciate their versatility.

1¹/₂ cups	dried green/brown lentils, rinsed	375 mL
2	red apples, skins on and chopped	2
1	stalk celery, chopped	1
³/₄ cup	pecans, chopped	175 mL
2 Tbsp	parsley, finely chopped	25 mL
Dressing:		
¹/₃ cup	vegetable oil	75 mL
2 tsp	Dijon mustard	10 mL
2 Tbsp	cider vinegar	25 mL
¹/₂ tsp	salt	2 mL

- In large saucepan, place lentils in 6 cups (1.5 L) water. Bring to boil, reduce heat, cover and simmer for 20-25 minutes until barely tender. Do not overcook. Drain and rinse in cold water.
- In tightly lidded jar, combine dressing ingredients. Shake well.
- In salad bowl add dressing to lentils. Toss well. Add other salad ingredients and mix. Chill in fridge for at least one hour before serving.

Serves 6-8.

Per Serving:
Protein . . . . *15 g*
Fat . . . . *21 g*
Carbohydrates . . . . *40 g*
Calories *392*
Dietary Fiber . . . . *6 g*

Tuscany Lentil Salad

Balsamic vinegar makes almost anything taste superb. It is especially delicious in dishes such as this lentil salad which conjures up the great flavors of Italy.

1 cup	dried green/brown lentils	250 mL
3 cups	water	750 mL
1	bay leaf	1
¹/₂ cup	white onion, finely chopped	125 mL
¹/₄ cup	green pepper, chopped	50 mL
¹/₂ cup	red pepper, chopped	125 mL
¹/₂ cup	carrots, coarsely chopped	125 mL
Dressing:		
2 Tbsp	olive oil	25 mL
3 Tbsp	balsamic vinegar	45 mL
1 tsp	sugar	5 mL
¹/₂ tsp	dry mustard	3 mL
1 tsp	dried basil (or 1 Tbsp/15 mL fresh)	5 mL
1	clove garlic, minced	1

- Rinse lentils. Place in saucepan with water and bay leaf. Cover and simmer for about 20-25 minutes until lentils are just tender (do not overcook or they will become mushy).
- Drain and rinse lentils. Discard bay leaf. Cool.
- In a large bowl, combine lentils with vegetables.
- In a tightly lidded jar, combine dressing ingredients. Shake well.
- Combine dressing with other ingredients and mix gently.
- Chill several hours (it is inclined to get soggy if left overnight). Serve on a bed of lettuce or spooned over a tossed salad.

Serves 6.

Per Serving:
Protein . . . . 8 g
Fat . . . . 4 g
Carbohydrates . . . . 23 g
Calories 160
Dietary Fiber . . . . 3 g

Orange White Bean Salad

This salad is so refreshing and eye-appealing, it will be a hit whenever you serve it. Be prepared to share the recipe – your guests will ask for it.

2¹/₂ cups	cooked navy, white kidney or Great Northern Beans*	625 mL
1	large orange, peeled and diced	1
1	green pepper, chopped	1
4	green onions, sliced including green parts	4
¹/₂ cup	fresh parsley, chopped	125 mL
Dressing:		
¹/₄ cup	vegetable oil	50 mL
3 Tbsp	white wine vinegar	45 mL
1 tsp	sugar	5 mL
¹/₂ tsp	Dijon mustard	3 mL

You can substitute 19 oz/540 mL of canned beans, drained and rinsed.

- Prepare 1 cup dried beans by quick-soak method on page 15. Cook according to chart on page 16. Be sure you don't overcook the beans. You want them tender but not mushy, so give them the "bite" test after 25 minutes.
- Drain, rinse and cool beans. Place in bowl and add the rest of the ingredients.
- In tightly lidded jar, combine dressing ingredients. Shake well. Add to bean mixture and stir gently.
- Chill in fridge for at least one hour.
- Serve in lettuce lined individual bowls, garnished with unpeeled orange slice twists.

Serves 6.

Per Serving:	
Protein	6 g
Fat	8 g
Carbohydrates	19 g
Calories	167
Dietary Fiber	7 g

Christmas Bean Salad

So named for obvious color reasons. However, it's too tasty to only serve during the festive season. Think about it in January when the Visa bill arrives – the salad works out to be pennies per serving.

3 cups	cooked navy or Great Northern beans*	750 mL
1	red pepper, chopped	1
1	green pepper, chopped	1
3	green onions, sliced (include green parts)	3
Dressing:		
½ cup	orange juice	125 mL
⅓ cup	balsamic vinegar	75 mL
1 Tbsp	dried basil or ¼ cup (50 mL) fresh, chopped	15 mL
	salt and pepper to taste	

Substitute 2 cans (14 oz/398 mL) white beans, drained and rinsed.

- Soak and cook 1⅓ cups (325 mL) beans as outlined on pages 15 and 16. Be sure not to overcook the beans. They should be tender but not mushy.
- Cool beans. In bowl, combine beans, peppers and onions.
- In tightly lidded jar, combine dressing ingredients. Shake well.
- Add dressing to bean mixture. Stir.
- Chill in fridge for at least 2 hours.
- Serve in lettuce lined salad bowl.

Serves 6.

You can also heap the bean mixture on thickly sliced tomatoes if you want individual portions.

Per Serving:	
Protein	7 g
Fat	0 g
Carbohydrates	23 g
Calories	119
Dietary Fiber	8 g

Main Dishes

Vegetarian Chili

The secret to the fresh taste of this chili is the lemon juice and not over-cooking it. If you don't have a meatless chili in your repertoire, this is the one. Adjust the seasonings to your taste.

3 Tbsp	vegetable oil	45 mL
2	large white onions, chopped	2
3	cloves garlic, minced	3
2	green peppers, chopped	2
1	can (28 oz/796 mL) diced tomatoes	1
4	small zucchini, sliced 1/4" (1 cm) thick	4
1	can (19 oz/540 mL) chick pea (garbanzo beans), drained and rinsed	1
1	can (19 oz/540mL) kidney beans, drained and rinsed	1
1 Tbsp	each chili powder, ground cumin, dried basil, dried oregano	15 mL
1 tsp	salt	5 ml
1 tsp	pepper	5 mL
1/2 cup	fresh parsley, chopped	125 mL
1/4 cup	lemon juice (fresh if possible)	50 mL

- In skillet, sauté onions, peppers and garlic in oil over medium heat for 5 minutes.
- Transfer to large, top-of-the-stove pot and add tomatoes and zucchini. Cook, uncovered, for 30 minutes.
- Stir in chick peas, kidney beans, spices, herbs, parsley and lemon juice. Cook for 15 minutes more.
- Serve in large bowls.

Serves 6-8.

Per Serving:	
Protein	15 g
Fat	10 g
Carbohydrates	54 g
Calories	345
Dietary Fiber	16 g

Champion Black Bean Chili

So called because after losing the first game of an 8-team summer cottage volleyball tournament, our group tucked into heaping bowls of this chili. To the chant of "bean power!" from our supporters, our team didn't lose another game and the championship was ours.

2 cups	dried black beans	500 mL
6 cups	water	1.5 L
4	bay leaves	4
3	cloves garlic, minced	3
2	large onions, chopped	2
3 Tbsp	vegetable oil	45 mL
1	can (28 oz/796 mL) diced tomatoes	1
1/2 cup	water	125 mL
2	fresh jalapeno peppers, minced	2
2 Tbsp	chili powder (more if desired)	25 mL
1 tsp	salt	5 mL
2 tsp	ground cumin (more if desired)	10 mL
1 Tbsp	dried oregano	15 mL
1 cup	red wine	250 mL
1/2 cup	fresh cilantro or parsley, chopped	125 mL

- Soak beans using quick-soak method on page 15. Drain and rinse.
- In large pot, place beans and cover with 3 inches (7.5 cm) water. Bring to boil, reduce heat, cover and simmer until tender, about 30 minutes. Drain and rinse.
- While beans are cooking, in skillet sauté onions and garlic in oil over medium heat. Add tomatoes, water, peppers, spices and oregano.
- Add skillet mixture to beans. Simmer 25 minutes. The mixture should be loose but not runny. Add a little liquid if necessary.
- Add wine and cilantro and continue to simmer another 10 minutes. Taste, adjust seasonings if necessary.
- Serve in individual bowls accompanied by slices of French bread.

Per Serving:
Protein . . . . 16 g
Fat . . . . 8 g
Carbohydrates . . . . 54 g
Calories 363
Dietary Fiber . . . . 28 g

Seafood Chili

The beauty of this simple recipe is you can use any white fish. Our suggestions are sole, cod, red snapper, halibut, turbot or any light-fleshed fish you are presented with by your fishing friends.

1 lb	white fish of your choice	450 g
3 Tbsp	vegetable oil	45 mL
2	large onions, chopped	2
1	yellow pepper, chopped	1
1	green pepper, chopped	1
1 cup	celery, chopped	250 mL
2	cloves garlic, minced	2
1	can (28 oz/796 mL) diced tomatoes	1
1	can (19 oz/540 mL) kidney beans, drained and rinsed	1
1/2 cup	fresh parsley	125 mL
1 tsp	chili powder (more if desired)	5 mL
	salt and pepper to taste	

- In large skillet, sauté onions, peppers, celery and garlic in oil over medium heat for 5 minutes.
- Transfer into large pot and add the remaining ingredients except the fish. Cover and simmer for 30 minutes.
- Cut fish into 1" (2.5 cm) pieces and add to pot. Simmer for another 15 minutes.

Serves 4.

Per Serving:
Protein .... 30 g
Fat .... 12 g
Carbohydrates .... 39 g
Calories 377
Dietary Fiber .... 13 g

Snow Chili

A quiet, unobtrusive dish, this chili may not be an instant attention-grabber. However, it is surprisingly tasty. Dress it up with fresh cilantro and serve it with warm crusty bread. This is a great way to use up left-over chicken.

1	large onion, chopped	1
3	cloves garlic, minced	3
3 Tbsp	vegetable oil	45 mL
2 cups	cooked chicken or turkey (more if desired)	500 mL
3 cups	chicken stock*	750 mL
2	cans (19 oz/540 mL) Great Northern Beans, navy or white kidney beans**, drained and rinsed	2
1 tsp	ground red chilies	5 mL
1/4 tsp	ground cloves, optional	1 mL
1 Tbsp	dried basil	15 mL
1/4 cup	fresh cilantro, chopped	50 mL

Can use bouillon cubes or instant granules. Follow package directions.
**If using dried beans, soak and cook 2 cups according to pages 15 & 16.*

- In large saucepan, sauté onion and garlic in oil over medium heat until tender but not brown.
- Add rest of ingredients except cilantro and simmer 40 minutes, stirring occasionally. If chili becomes too thick or dry during cooking, add more chicken stock.
- About 5 minutes before serving, add cilantro.

Serves 6.

Per Serving:	
Protein	23 g
Fat	10 g
Carbohydrates	28 g
Calories	291
Dietary Fiber	11 g

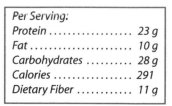

Chipotle Chili

The basic chili recipe goes south of the border with the addition of smokey jalapenos peppers (chipotle), black beans, beer and fresh lime juice. Gourmet in taste and flavor, this recipe is just as easy to make as your basic chili.

1 lb	ground beef	450 g
1 Tbsp	vegetable oil	15 mL
1	large onion, chopped	1
2	cloves garlic, minced	2
1	can (19 oz/540 mL) kidney beans, drained & rinsed	1
1	can (19 oz/540 mL) black beans, drained & rinsed	1
1	can (28 oz/798 mL) crushed tomatoes	1
1	bottle (12 oz/340 mL) honey lager beer	1
1 tsp	chipotle pepper in adobo sauce, finely chopped	5 mL
1 Tbsp	chili powder	15 mL
1 tsp	salt	5 mL
1 cup	sour cream	250 mL
1 Tbsp	lime juice	15 mL

- In a large pot, sauté beef until the pink is gone. Remove from pan.
- Add oil and sauté onions and garlic over medium heat for 5 minutes.
- Add meat and rest of the ingredients. Simmer for one hour.
- Combine sour cream and lime juice.
- Serve in large bowls with a spoonful of the sour cream mixture on top of each serving.

Serves 6.

Per Serving:
Protein . . . . .26 g
Fat . . . . .20 g
Carbohydrates . . . . .44 g
Calories 465
Dietary Fiber . . . . .11 g

Black-eyed Pea Chili

Confusion reigns among recipe writers, bean producers, bulk food store owners and supermarket packagers. What is the novice bean buyer to think when he/she sees the same pulse (a generic name for edible legumes) labeled a "bean" in one outlet and just down the street it's a "pea"? One bulk food owner confided that she orders them as black-eyed *beans* and puts them in a bin marked black-eyed *peas* ! The short answer is yes, they are beans but they don't need presoaking.

1¼ cup	dried black-eyed peas	300 mL
3 cups	water	750 mL
1	whole boneless, skinned chicken breast, cut in 1" (2.5 cm) pieces	1
1	large onion, chopped	1
2 Tbsp	vegetable oil	25 mL
3	cloves garlic, minced	3
1	can (28 oz/798 mL) diced tomatoes	1
1	green pepper	1
2 Tbsp	chili powder	25 mL
	salt and pepper to taste	
½ tsp	red pepper sauce (optional)	2 mL

- In a large covered pot, simmer the beans in 3 cups of water for 30-40 minutes until soft but not mushy. Do not drain.
- Meanwhile, in skillet, sauté chicken pieces, onion and garlic in oil until chicken loses pink colour. Add chicken mixture and remaining ingredients to beans. Stir well.
- Simmer uncovered for 20 minutes. Adjust thickness of mixture by adding more water or tomato juice if necessary. Chili should be "loose" but not "runny" or you have just made another pot of soup!
- Taste and add salt, pepper and pepper sauce if desired.

Serves 4.

Per Serving:
Protein . . . . .13 g
Fat . . . . 5 g
Carbohydrates . . . . .18 g
Calories 157
Dietary Fiber . . . . 5 g

Burritos, Wraps & Roll-ups

What is the difference? Well, we think that a wrap and a roll-up are the same thing though "wrap" seems to be the most popular name. A wrap is a filled tortilla (or roti) which is rolled so it can be eaten by hand. You can use any number of leftover bean dishes as the basis for a wrap. There are now a variety of tortillas (plain, whole wheat, spinach and tomato). Also try a roti if you are using a "dahl" as a filling. A burrito is also a filled tortilla, but is eaten with a knife and fork and condiments, such as salsa and sour cream, are put on top of the rolled tortilla (with a wrap, condiments are put on top of the filling inside the tortilla).

Whatever the name, you can add rice, fried leftover potatoes, tomatoes and a variety of cheeses. The most common condiments are salsa and sour cream but to make a taste difference try chipotle mayonnaise (recipe below), sprouts, hot sauce or sesame seeds. On the next few pages we've given you some some suggestions for wraps and burritos you can make. Enjoy.

Chipotle Mayonnaise

This is a "must" addition to wraps or burritos or as a dip for veggies. Be sure to refrigerate before using so it "sets up". It keeps well in the fridge.

²/₃ cup	real Mayonnaise	150 mL
¹/₃ cup	sour cream	75 mL
2 – 4	chipotle peppers*	2 – 4
1 tsp	adobo sauce*	5 mL
2 tsp	lime juice	10 mL
1 tsp	ground cumin	5 mL
	salt and pepper to taste	

Buy a can of chipotle peppers in adobo sauce. After opening put in a tightly sealed jar and refrigerate. It will keep for a long time.

■ Combine all ingredients in a food processor and blend until smooth. Refrigerate for at least 2 hours before serving.

Per Serving:
Protein .... 0 g
Fat ....11 g
Carbohydrates .... 3 g
Calories 113
Dietary Fiber .... 0 g

Yields 1 cup.

Chicken & Goat Cheese Burrito

If you want a gourmet burrito, this fits the bill. It is only slightly more work, but definitely worth the effort. You need to have Black Bean Hummus (page 25) on hand.

2 Tbsp	vegetable oil	25 mL
1	boneless, skinned chicken breast	1
2 tsp	cumin	10 mL
4 oz	goat cheese, crumbled	110 g
1½ cup	Black Bean Hummus (page 25)	375 mL
4	spinach tortillas	4
	mixed greens or sunflower sprouts	
	salsa and sour cream	

- Cut chicken in 3" (1 cm x 6 cm) strips. Coat with cumin.
- In skillet, heat oil over medium heat. Brown chicken until cooked, about 5-10 minutes.
- While chicken is cooking, wrap tortillas tightly in foil and heat in a 350°F (180°C) oven for 10 minutes.
- While still hot, top each piece of chicken with goat cheese.
- Spread tortillas with the black bean hummus. Place chicken toward one edge.
- Top with mixed greens or sunflower sprouts
- Fold bottom edge of tortilla over chicken. Roll up tightly. Serve with salsa and sour cream.

Serves 4.

Per Serving:
Protein . . . . .26 g
Fat . . . . .22 g
Carbohydrates . . . . .45 g
Calories 474
Dietary Fiber . . . . 9 g

Bean & Veggie Burrito

This recipe uses leftover Baked Black Beans (page 112). You can be as imaginative as you like with the filling.

2 tsp	vegetable oil	10 mL
1	small onion, finely chopped	1
3	cloves garlic, minced	3
1/2	green pepper, thinly sliced	1/2
1/2	red or yellow pepper, thinly sliced	1/2
1	medium zucchini, cut in 1 1/2" (3.5 cm) strips	1
1/2 cup	mushrooms, sliced	125 mL
1 tsp	dried oregano	5 mL
2 tsp	chili powder	10 mL
1 tsp	ground cumin	5 mL
3/4 cup	cooked rice (optional)	175 mL
6	flour tortilla	6
2 cups	Baked Black Beans (page 112)	500 mL
1/2 cup	Monterey Jack cheese, grated	125 mL
6 Tbsp	salsa	90 mL
6 Tbsp	low fat sour cream	90 mL

- In skillet, sauté onion in oil over medium heat for 2 minutes. Add garlic and vegetables. Cook, stirring often until vegetables are just tender.
- Add oregano, chili and cumin and, if desired, cooked rice. Mix well.
- While vegetable mixture is cooking, wrap tortillas tightly in foil. Heat in a 350°F (180°C) oven for 10 minutes.
- Spread warm tortilla with 1/3 cup (75 mL) of Baked Black Beans and 1/3 cup (75 mL) of vegetable mixture across each tortilla, just below the center. Top with cheese, salsa and sour cream.
- Fold bottom edge of tortilla over filling, fold in sides and roll up.
- If burritos are not desired temperature, place on a baking sheet, seam side down, and bake at 350°F (180°C) for 10 minutes.
- Serve with additional salsa and sour cream.

Serves 6.

Per Serving:
Protein . . . . .12 g
Fat . . . . 9 g
Carbohydrates . . . . .40 g
Calories 279
Dietary Fiber . . . . 6 g

Feta Veggie Wrap

Truly one of the fastest meals you may ever make, especially when you have extra Vegetable Chili in the freezer. Wraps like this one might turn out to be your favorite fast-food!

For each wrap you will need:		
1	10" (25 cm) tortilla	1
²/₃ cup	Vegetarian Chili (page 88)	150 mL
¹/₃ cup	brown basmati rice, cooked	75 mL
3 Tbsp	crumbled feta cheese	45 mL
	spinach or basil leaves	
1 Tbsp	each, sour cream and salsa	15 mL

- Wrap tortillas in foil and heat in 350ºF (180ºC) oven for 10 minutes.
- Heat Vegetable Chili and basmati rice until warm.
- For each wrap, place chili and rice on each tortilla. Crumble feta cheese over chili and rice.
- Place spinach or basil leaves on top. Add sour cream and salsa, if desired.
- To assemble wraps, fold up bottom and then roll from the side, add sour cream and salsa, and eat out of hand. If serving as a burrito, put on condiments on top after serving.
- If not the desired temperature, cover wraps completely in foil and place on baking sheet. Heat in a 350˚F (180˚C) oven for 10 minutes until warm (*alternate warming method:* wrap tortillas in paper towels and microwave 30 to 60 seconds until warm).

Makes one wrap.

Per Serving:	
Protein	18 g
Fat	20 g
Carbohydrates	61 g
Calories	484
Dietary Fiber	8 g

Black Bean Quesadillas

If you have leftover Baked Black Beans (page 112), this is a fast and easy luncheon dish. You can be imaginative with your fillings – one day when we ran out of the usual beans we used leftover Tuscany Lentil Salad and had a totally different taste treat.

1½ cups	Baked Black Beans (page 112)	375 mL
8	medium-size flour tortillas	8
¾ cup	mozzarella or Monterey Jack cheese, grated	175 mL
½ cup	medium salsa	125 mL
1 Tbsp	olive oil	15 mL

- Spread ¼ of the Baked Black Bean mixture onto 4 tortillas. Top each with ¼ of the cheese and salsa.
- Place remaining 4 tortillas on top, pressing them down gently. Brush both sides lightly with oil. Arrange on a baking sheet.
- Bake for 5 minutes at 350°F (180°C) or until lightly browned and cheese is melted. They can also be browned in a frying pan or on the barbecue.
- Cut into quarters.

Serves 4 for lunch.

Per Serving:	
Protein	18 g
Fat	18 g
Carbohydrates	71 g
Calories	513
Dietary Fiber	13 g

Dahl Wrap

Roti might be described as an East Indian tortilla. They have a very interesting flavor and are great served with Yellow Split Pea Dahl (page 120) or Red Lentil Dahl (page 121). You may have to ask for roti, as they are not as common as tortillas in the supermarkets, and seem to be available only in an 8 inch (20 cm) size. You will likely need two for each person.

For each roti you will need:		
1/2 cup	dahl (Yellow Split Pea Dahl (page 120) or Red Lentil Dahl (page 121)	125 mL
1/4 cup	cooked brown rice	50 mL
1	8" (20 cm) roti	1
	toasted sesame seeds (optional)	

- Heat dahl and brown rice until warm.
- Wrap rotis in foil and heat in a 350°F (180°C) oven for 10 minutes.
- Place dahl and rice in center of each roti. Add sesame seeds on top.
- To assemble wraps, fold up bottom and then roll from the side and eat out of hand.
- If not the desired temperature, cover completely in foil and place on baking sheet. Heat in a 350°F (180°C) oven for 10 minutes until warm (*alternate warming method:* wrap tortillas in paper towels and microwave 30 to 60 seconds until warm).

Makes one wrap.

Only about 4% of the calories in legumes (except soybeans and chick peas) come from fat.

Per Serving:
Protein . . . . .11 g
Fat . . . . 6 g
Carbohydrates . . . . .60 g
Calories 331
Dietary Fiber . . . . 5 g

Santa Fe Lentil Wrap

Hopefully you stashed away some leftover Mexican Lentil Casserole (page 115) in the freezer so that you can whip up this satisfying wrap when time is tight at lunch or dinner.

For each wrap you will need:		
1	10" (25 cm) tortilla	1
1 cup	Mexican Lentil Casserole (page 115)	250 mL
1/4 cup	Monterey Jack cheese	50 mL
	sour cream and salsa	

- Heat Mexican Lentil Casserole until warm.
- Cover the tortillas completely in foil and place on baking sheet. Heat in a 350°F (180°C) oven for 10 minutes.
- For each wrap, place lentil mixture on each tortilla. Top with Monterey cheese. Add sour cream and salsa, if desired.
- To assemble wraps, fold up bottom and then roll from the side and eat out of hand. If serving as a burrito, put sour cream and salsa on top after serving.

Makes one wrap.

Per Serving:
Protein . . . . .19 g
Fat . . . . .22 g
Carbohydrates . . . . .58 g
Calories 498
Dietary Fiber . . . . 5 g

Tortilla Treat

If you have Baked Black Beans (page 112) or Champion Black Bean Chili (page 89) on hand, you can whip up this Mexican-inspired dish faster than making a tuna salad sandwich. Spend less than five minutes in the kitchen and you have a tasty lunch.

4	8" (20 cm) tortillas	4
2 cups	Baked Black Beans (page 112) or Champion Black Bean Chili (page 89)	500 mL
2	medium tomatoes, chopped	2
4	green onions, finely chopped	4
1 cup	grated cheddar or Monterey Jack cheese	250 mL

- Spread 1/2 cup (125 mL) of baked black beans on each tortilla.
- Top with chopped tomatoes and green onions. Sprinkle with grated cheese.
- Place on cookie sheet and bake in 350°F (180°C) oven for 10-15 minutes.
- Top with salsa before serving for a spicier version.

Serves 4.

Per Serving:	
Protein	19 g
Fat	17 g
Carbohydrates	45 g
Calories	399
Dietary Fiber	7 g

Skillet Chili Chicken

A complete meal in a pan. Accompanied by your favorite bread, you're home at 5:30 and sitting down by 6:15, thanks to instant rice and canned beans. It is a mild chili dish, so feel free to add more spice and hot pepper sauce.

1 lb	boneless chicken breasts, cut in 6 pieces	450 g
1 Tbsp	vegetable oil	15 mL
1	medium onion, chopped	1
1	green pepper, chopped	1
3	cloves garlic, minced	3
1	can (19 oz/540 mL) kidney beans, drained	1
1	can (14 oz/398 mL) diced tomatoes	1
2 tsp	chili powder	10 mL
3/4 cup	instant rice or 1 cup (250 mL) cooked rice	175 mL
3	dashes, hot pepper sauce (e.g. Tabasco)	3
3/4 cup	Monterey Jack cheese, shredded	175 mL

- In skillet, lightly brown chicken in oil until pink is no longer evident. Remove and set aside.
- Add more oil if necessary and sauté onion, pepper and garlic until tender for 5 minutes.
- Stir in kidney beans, chili powder and tomatoes. Add rice and pepper sauce.
- Arrange chicken pieces on top of mixture. Cover and simmer for 20 minutes.
- Top with shredded cheese and simmer 5 more minutes until cheese melts.

Serves 4.

Per Serving:
Protein . . . . .40 g
Fat . . . . .12 g
Carbohydrates . . . . .41 g
Calories 432
Dietary Fiber . . . . .10 g

Moroccan Chicken

There is always a recipe that fights its way to the front of the line, and this is definitely the one. Beloved by all, it can be dressed up or down. For the family, serve over rice. Special occasions demand the exotic twist of raisins and couscous. It's easily doubled.

2 Tbsp	olive oil	25 mL
2	boneless, skinned chicken beasts, cut in 1/2	2
1	medium onion, chopped	1
1	can (14 oz/398 mL) diced tomatoes	1
1	medium zucchini, halved lengthwise and sliced 1/4" (.5 cm) thick	1
1 tsp	dried oregano	5 mL
2 tsp	ground cumin (more if desired)	10 mL
1/2 tsp	ground cinnamon	3 mL
	salt to taste	
1 cup	canned chick peas, drained and rinsed	250 mL
2 Tbsp	raisins (optional)	25 mL
1 1/2 cups	cooked rice or couscous*	375 mL

*To cook couscous, bring 1 1/2 cups (375 mL) water to boil in medium saucepan. Add 3/4 cup (175 mL) of couscous, turn off heat, cover, and let stand for 5 minutes. Fluff up with a fork.

- In skillet, heat oil over medium heat. Brown chicken on both sides. Remove chicken from pan.
- Add onion and sauté until tender for about 5 minutes. Add tomatoes.
- Return chicken to skillet and simmer, covered in tomato mixture for 25-35 minutes.
- Stir in zucchini, oregano and spices. Cover and simmer for 5 minutes until zucchini is almost tender.
- Add chick peas and raisins. Heat through, about 5 minutes.
- Serve over rice or couscous.

Serves 4.

Per Serving:
Protein . . . . .34 g
Fat . . . . 9 g
Carbohydrates . . . . .43 g
Calories 387
Dietary Fiber . . . . 5 g

Salsa Chicken

A busy executive gave us this chicken and kidney bean recipe. Just as good for fish (recipe below) but using black beans.

1	can (19 oz/540 mL) red kidney beans	1
2	boneless, skinned chicken breasts, cut in 1/2	2
1 cup	medium or hot salsa	250 mL

- Drain and rinse kidney beans. Place on the bottom of an ungreased casserole dish.
- Put the four chicken pieces on the beans. Cover with the salsa.
- Bake, covered, at 350°F (180°C) for 40 minutes.

Serves 4.

Per Serving:
Protein . . . . .35 g
Fat . . . . 2 g
Carbohydrates . . . . .23 g
Calories 253
Dietary Fiber . . . . 9 g

Salsa Fish

1	can (14 oz/396 mL) black beans*	1
1 1/2 lbs	white fish (cod or red snapper are best)	550 g
1 cup	medium or hot salsa	250 mL

- Drain and rinse kidney beans. Place on the bottom of an ungreased casserole dish.
- Put the fish on the beans. Cover with the salsa.
- Bake, covered, at 350°F (180°C) for 15-20 minutes, depending on the thickness of the fish.

Serves 4.

Per Serving:
Protein . . . . .34 g
Fat . . . . 2 g
Carbohydrates . . . . .27 g
Calories 258
Dietary Fiber . . . . 7 g

Garbanzo Stew

Serve this as a main course or as an accompaniment to beef or pork. For a one-dish meal, you can put pork chops on the top of the stew and cook them with the vegetables. Seriously delicious!

2 cups	cooked rice	500 mL
1	can (19oz/540 mL) garbanzo beans (chick peas), drained and rinsed	1
4	potatoes, quartered and thinly sliced	4
6	carrots, thinly sliced	6
2	medium onions, quartered and thinly sliced	2
2 cups	beef or vegetable broth *	500 mL
1/2 cup	chopped cilantro or parsley	125 mL
1 tsp	cumin	5 mL
1/4 tsp	red pepper flakes	1 mL

* Can use bouillon cubes or instant granules. Follow package instructions.

- In a medium-sized casserole dish, combine all ingredients.
- Bake, covered, at 350°F (180°C) for 45 minutes or until vegetables are tender.
- Serve in a warmed bowl with a hearty bread.

Serves 4.

Per Serving:
Protein . . . . .15 g
Fat . . . . 3 g
Carbohydrates . . . . .92 g
Calories 445
Dietary Fiber . . . . .11 g

Quick Spicy Sausage Stew

There are lots of tasty sausage on the market these days. It's up to your palate how much fire you can handle. Remember, there's salsa in this recipe as well.

1 lb	spicy sausage, cut in 1/2" (1 cm) slices	450 g
1 Tbsp	vegetable oil	15 mL
1	large onion, chopped	1
2	cloves garlic, minced	2
1	green pepper, chopped	1
1	can (28 oz/796 mL) diced tomatoes	1
1	can (14 oz/398 mL) kidney beans, drained and rinsed	1
1 cup	canned chick peas (garbanzo beans), drained and rinsed	250 mL
1/2 cup	salsa, medium strength	125 mL
1 tsp	ground cumin	5 mL
1 tsp	dried oregano	5 mL

- In large skillet, brown sausage in oil over medium heat. Remove from pan. Drain fat, leaving a small amount, to brown onion and garlic for 5 minutes.
- Return sausage to pan. Add rest of ingredients, cover and simmer for 20 minutes.

Serves 4-6.

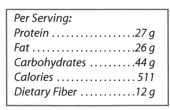

Per Serving:
Protein . . . . 27 g
Fat . . . . 26 g
Carbohydrates . . . . 44 g
Calories 511
Dietary Fiber . . . . 12 g

Cowboy Casserole

An easy, quick dinner casserole. Make it the day before, tuck it in the fridge and then slip it into the oven when you return home from work. Dieticians approve of the combination of beans and rice.

1 lb	ground beef	450 g
1	onion, chopped	1
2	cloves garlic, minced	2
1 tsp	chili powder	5 mL
1	can (28 oz/796 mL) diced tomatoes	1
1 cup	uncooked instant rice or 1½ cups (300 mL) cooked rice	250mL
1	can (14 oz/398 mL) kidney beans drained and rinsed	1
1 cup	cheddar cheese, grated	250 mL

- In skillet, brown beef, onion and garlic over medium heat. Drain fat.
- Transfer mixture to oven-proof casserole and stir in remaining ingredients except cheese.
- Bake, covered, for 40 minutes at 350°F (180°C). Uncover, sprinkle with grated cheese. Return to oven and bake, uncovered, for 10 minutes more or until cheese is melted.

Serves 4-6.

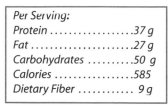

Per Serving:
Protein ....37 g
Fat ....27 g
Carbohydrates ....50 g
Calories 585
Dietary Fiber .... 9 g

Robinson Crusoe

This layered casserole has been in our family for so many years the origins of its name has become a mystery. Perhaps the famous castaway had only one pot on the island for cooking dinner.

2 cups	potatoes, peeled and sliced	500 mL
2 cups	celery, chopped	500 mL
1 lb	ground beef	450 g
1 Tbsp	Worcestershire sauce	15 mL
1/2 tsp each	salt and pepper	3 mL
1	large onion, sliced	1
1	large green pepper, sliced	1
1	can (19 oz/540 mL) kidney beans, drained and rinsed	1
1	can (19 oz/540 mL) diced tomatoes	1
1 tsp each	dried thyme and oregano	5 mL each

- In a large casserole, arrange the potatoes on the bottom of the dish. Sprinkle with salt and pepper.
- Layer the celery followed by a layer of uncooked ground beef. Sprinkle with Worcestershire sauce.
- Add onions, green pepper and kidney beans in separate layers. Sprinkle with thyme and oregano.
- Top with the canned tomatoes. Cover and cook at 350°F (180°C) for 1-1 1/2 hours.

Serves 6.

Per Serving:	
Protein	21 g
Fat	16 g
Carbohydrates	36 g
Calories	367
Dietary Fiber	8 g

Tortilla Stack

We think of this as Mexican lasagne where tortillas replace the pasta. For great party fare, double the recipe, leave the tortillas whole and place in a springform pan instead of an 8" x 8" pan. Serve at the table, cut in wedges and your guests will be impressed.

2 tsp	vegetable oil	10 mL
1	small onion, finely chopped	1
1	green pepper, finely chopped	1
1	clove garlic, minced	1
1	jalapeno pepper, minced	1
1 tsp	dried oregano	5 mL
1	can (14 oz/398 mL) tomato sauce	1
1½ cups	cooked black beans*	375 mL
½ cup	kernel corn, canned or fresh	125 mL
3 or 4	large tortillas	3 or 4
1½ cups	grated cheddar or Monterey Jack cheese	375 mL

*If using dried beans, soak and cook ¾ of a cup (125 mL), following instructions on page 15 and 16.

- In a large saucepan, sauté onion, green pepper, garlic and jalapeno pepper in oil over medium heat for 5 minutes.
- Add other ingredients except tortillas and cheese. Simmer, covered, for 30 minutes. Add more liquid if getting dry. Mash the bean mixture against the sides of the saucepan to obtain a smoother consistency.
- Lightly oil an 8"x8" (20 cm x 20 cm) pan.
- Cut tortillas in 1" (2.5 cm) strips and place a single layer in the bottom of pan.
- Spoon on ⅓ of the bean mixture, then ⅓ of the cheese. Repeat layers twice.
- Cover with foil and bake at 375°F (190°C) for 25 minutes or until hot. If desired, serve with light sour cream and salsa.

Serves 4.

Per Serving:	
Protein	23 g
Fat	21 g
Carbohydrates	54 g
Calories	486
Dietary Fiber	8 g

Use gloves when chopping Jalapeno peppers. Discard seeds.

Mexican Brunch

The perk in taking a Mexican vacation in the middle of writing a cookbook was the discovery of a totally unexpected recipe. Described verbally in a square in Puerto Vallarta, it sounded delicious and so it proved to be.

2	medium tortillas	2
1/2 cup	refried beans*	125 mL
4	eggs	4
1/2 cup	milk	125 mL
2 tsp	butter or margarine	10 mL
	salsa	

Use canned or make your own. Recipe on page 135.

- Place tortillas on baking sheet and cover with refried beans. Warm in 325°F (160°C) oven for 5 to 10 minutes.
- Meanwhile, in medium bowl, beat eggs and milk.
- In skillet, melt butter over low heat. Add eggs and stir frequently until creamy but not dry.
- Serve immediately accompanied with salsa.

Serves 2.

Per Serving:
Protein . . . . .23 g
Fat . . . . .27 g
Carbohydrates . . . . .45 g
Calories 506
Dietary Fiber . . . . 6 g

Enchiladas

These are easy to make if you have some Black Bean Chili (page 89) or Baked Black Beans (page 112) on hand to use for filling. We think you'll find them as good as any meat-filled enchiladas.

8	medium-sized flour tortillas	8
3 cups	Black Bean Chili or Baked Black Beans*	750 mL
	Enchilada Sauce (recipe follows)	
1 cup	cheddar or Monterey Jack cheese, grated	250 mL
Enchilada Sauce:		
2 tsp	vegetable oil	10 mL
1	medium onion, finely chopped	1
2	cans (14 oz/398 mL) tomato sauce	2
1/2 cup	water	125 mL
2 tsp	chili powder (more if desired)	10 mL
1/2 tsp	ground cumin (more if desired)	3 mL
1/2 tsp	oregano	3 mL

Recipes found on page 89 and 112.

- To make sauce, sauté onion in oil in medium saucepan over medium heat for 5 minutes. Add other sauce ingredients, cover and simmer for 30 minutes.
- To assemble: warm tortillas slightly so that they roll more easily. In a lightly oiled 9"x13" (22cm x 33cm) pan, cover the bottom with a thin layer of enchilada sauce.
- Put about 1/3 cup (75 mL) of Black Bean Chili in a strip down the middle of each tortilla. Top with 1 Tbsp (15 mL) of cheese. Roll tortilla around filling and place seam side down in a single layer in the baking pan.
- Cover tortillas completely with remaining sauce. Sprinkle with the rest of the cheese. Bake at 350°F (180°C) for 20 to 25 minutes.

Makes 8 enchiladas.

Per Serving:	
Protein	14 g
Fat	13 g
Carbohydrates	39 g
Calories	316
Dietary Fiber	4 g

Baked Black Beans

Black beans have now elbowed navy beans off center stage. This casse-role is today's answer to your grandmother's Boston Baked Bean recipe. Make lots so it can be used in your quesadillas, burritos and enchiladas.

2 cups	dried black beans	500 mL
1/4 lb	bacon, cut in narrow strips (optional)	100 g
2 Tbsp	vegetable oil	25 mL
1	large green pepper, chopped	1
1	large onion, chopped	1
3	cloves garlic, minced	3
1	can (4 oz/114 mL) diced green chilies	1
1/2 cup	sherry *	125 mL
1 Tbsp	ground cumin	15 mL
1	can (14 oz/398 mL) tomato sauce	1
1/4 cup	fresh cilantro, finely chopped	50 mL

* Red wine can be substituted.

- Soak beans using quick-soak method page 15. Drain and rinse.
- In large saucepan, place beans and cover with 3" (7.5 cm) water. Bring to boil, reduce heat, cover and simmer until tender, about 30 minutes. Drain and rinse.
- In skillet, cook bacon until crisp. Remove from pan. Drain fat.
- In the same skillet, add oil and sauté green pepper, onion and garlic until tender, about 5 minutes.
- Place all ingredients in a large casserole and bake, covered, at 325°F (160°C) for 1 hour. Check occasionally and add liquid if necessary.

Serves 6.

Per Serving:
Protein . . . . .15 g
Fat . . . . 5 g
Carbohydrates . . . . .51 g
Calories 320
Dietary Fiber . . . . .28 g

Many Baked Beans

This recipe could also be called the NAFTA Casserole. Representative beans from Canada, Mexico and the USA are all in the same pot, simmering together. Hopefully, NAFTA's results will be as satisfying as this dish.

1/2 cup	each, dried black beans, navy beans, kidney beans (or small red beans) and pinto beans	125 mL
1/4 lb	bacon, cut in matchstick pieces	100 g
2	medium onions, chopped	2
1	green pepper, chopped	1
1 tsp	allspice	5 mL
2 Tbsp	light molasses	25 mL
2 Tbsp	brown sugar	25 mL
1 Tbsp	tomato ketchup	15 mL
1 tsp	dry mustard	5 mL
1 Tbsp	soy sauce	15 mL
1	can (14 oz/398 mL) tomato sauce	1
1 cup	water	250 mL
	juice of one lemon	

- Combine beans. Rinse. Soak beans using quick-soak method on page 15. Drain.
- In large saucepan, place beans and cover with 3" (7.5 cm) water. Bring to boil, reduce heat, cover and simmer for 40 minutes. Drain and rinse.
- While beans are cooking, fry bacon in a large skillet until crisp. Remove from skillet. Sauté onions and green pepper in bacon fat for 5 minutes.
- Add bacon and remaining ingredients. Simmer for 5 minutes more.
- In large lightly greased casserole, combine beans and tomato mixture.
- Bake, covered, at 325°F (160°C) for 1-1 1/2 hours, checking occasionally and adding liquid if necessary.

Serves 6.

Per Serving:	
Protein	16 g
Fat	10 g
Carbohydrates	56 g
Calories	372
Dietary Fiber	27 g

Quick Southern Pizza

A change of taste from the usual pizza. Can be assembled in five minutes if you use the pre-made bread shells or pizza crusts featured in supermarkets. The sauce can be kept in the fridge for at least a week and freezes well.

Black Bean Sauce: *

1	can (14 oz/398 mL) black beans, drained and rinsed	1
1	can (4 oz/114 mL) green chilies, undrained	1
1	clove garlic, minced	1
1/2 tsp	ground cumin	3 mL
	pizza crust, your choice of size	

* Can also use Black Bean Hummus as the base, page 25.

- Combine beans and undrained chilies in blender or food processor. Blend for a few seconds. Add rest of ingredients and blend until smooth. Use immediately or keep in fridge to use as a base for your pizzas.

Yield: 1 1/2 cups (375 mL)

- First spread the black bean sauce generously over the pizza and top with any of the following combinations:
  - Shrimp, chopped green onions, crumbled feta cheese.
  - Sliced mushrooms, diced canned green chilies, grated Havarti or Cheddar cheese.
  - Chopped, seeded tomatoes, green pepper, grated Monterey Jack.
- Bake in the oven following the pizza crust directions.

Per Serving:	
Protein	15 g
Fat	2 g
Carbohydrates	79 g
Calories	402
Dietary Fiber	7 g

Mexican Lentil Casserole

Even if lentils have not been your favorite food, we feel you will be won over by this recipe. No problem with leftovers – use them for filling wraps or quesadillas.

2 Tbsp	vegetable oil	25 mL
1	medium onion, chopped	1
1	medium green pepper, chopped	1
3	stalks celery, chopped	3
4 cups	water	1 L
1 cup	dried green/brown lentils	250 mL
1½ cups	cooked rice (brown is nice)	375 mL
1	can (5.5 oz/156 mL) tomato paste	1
1	pkg (1¼ oz/39 mL) taco seasoning mix	1
1 tsp	chili powder, more if desired	5 mL
½ cup	crushed taco chips (optional)	125 mL
½ cup	cheddar or Monterey Jack cheese, grated	125 mL

- In large saucepan, sauté onions, green peppers and celery in oil over medium heat for 5 minutes.
- Add water and bring to boil. Stir in lentils. Cover, reduce heat and simmer for 40 minutes. Do not drain.
- In medium-sized, lightly oiled casserole dish, combine lentils with other ingredients except taco chips and cheese. Bake, uncovered, for 20 minutes at 350°F (180°C).
- Sprinkle taco chips and cheese on top. Bake another 5 minutes or until cheese melts.

Serves 6.

```
Per Serving:
Protein . . . . . . . . . . . . . . . . .13 g
Fat . . . . . . . . . . . . . . . . . . . . . 8 g
Carbohydrates . . . . . . . . . .40 g
Calories . . . . . . . . . . . . . . . .278
Dietary Fiber . . . . . . . . . . . . 5 g
```

Italian Pasta & Beans

There are many recipes for this traditional Italian dish, *Paste e Fagioli*. This is our version – quick and inexpensive.

3 Tbsp	olive oil	45 mL
2	cloves garlic, minced	2
1	can (19 oz/540 mL) diced tomatoes	1
½ cup	fresh parsley, chopped	125 mL
1 tsp	dried basil	5 mL
1 tsp	dried oregano	5 mL
	salt and pepper to taste	
1 cup	cooked kidney beans (red or white)*	250 mL
1 cup	penne or fettucine pasta	250 mL
	freshly grated parmesan cheese	

* If using dried beans, prepare ½ cup (125 mL) according to soaking and cooking instructions on pages 15 and 16.

- In medium saucepan, sauté garlic in oil over medium heat for 2 minutes. Add tomatoes, parsley, basil and oregano. Simmer for 15 minutes, breaking up the tomatoes.
- Add beans and simmer for 5 minutes. Taste and add salt and pepper as desired.
- Cook pasta according to package directions. Keep warm.
- Place warm pasta in a heated bowl. Cover with sauce. Toss well.
- Serve with parmesan cheese.

Serves 4.

The real taste of parmesan cheese comes when it's freshly grated. Parmesan Reggiano is the most flavorful. If you buy it already grated, buy from the deli section where it has been grated and stored in the refrigerator.

Per Serving:
Protein . . . . .10 g
Fat . . . . .12 g
Carbohydrates . . . . .41 g
Calories 310
Dietary Fiber . . . . 7 g

Veggie Spaghetti Sauce

This family recipe has evolved over the years. Gradually the amount of ground beef has been reduced as more veggies have been added. Now chick peas have completely replaced the ground beef. Double the recipe to make Vegetarian Lasagne (page 118), and have some left for a simple spaghetti dinner. Freezes well.

1 Tbsp	vegetable oil	15 mL
1	large onion, finely chopped	1
2	cloves garlic, minced	2
1	green pepper, chopped	1
1	medium zucchini, chopped	1
1 cup	sliced mushrooms	250 mL
1	can (28 oz/796 mL) crushed tomatoes	1
2	cans (5.5 oz/156 mL) tomato paste	2
1	can (19 oz/540 mL) chick peas/ garbanzo beans, drained and rinsed	1
1 cup	water	250 mL
1 cup	red wine*	250 mL
1 tsp	paprika	5 mL
1 tsp	each, dried basil and oregano	5 mL
½ tsp	each, thyme and allspice	3 mL
8 drops	hot red pepper sauce (e.g. Tabasco)	8 drops
	salt and pepper to taste	

Can substitute water or stock, but wine is the best.

- In soup pot, sauté onion, garlic and green pepper in oil over medium heat for 5 minutes. Add zucchini and mushrooms. Cook 3 minutes.
- Partially mash the chick peas.
- Add tomatoes, tomato paste, chick peas and liquid. Simmer, partially covered, for 40 minutes. Stir occasionally.
- Add herbs and spices and cook 15 minutes more.
- Serve over cooked spaghetti. Sprinkle with grated parmesan cheese.

Per Serving:
Protein . . . . .11 g
Fat . . . . 5 g
Carbohydrates . . . . .45 g
Calories 276
Dietary Fiber . . . . .10 g

Yields 6 cups.

Vegetarian Lasagne

Do you hesitate to make lasagne because it is too time consuming? With spaghetti sauce on hand and the oven-ready lasagne noodles, it takes less than 15 minutes to assemble.

8 cups	Veggie Spaghetti Sauce (previous page)	2 L
	(double the recipe, and reserve 4 cups for future use)	
12	oven-ready lasagne noodles*	12
10 oz	mozzarella cheese	300 g
16 oz	light cottage cheese	500 g
1	egg, beaten	1
1/2 cup	freshly grated parmesan cheese	125 mL

Can use fresh if available. Just ask for enough to make 3 layers.

- Thinly slice the mozzarella cheese.
- In bowl, blend cottage cheese and eggs.
- In a deep 9"x13" (22cm x 33cm) baking dish, spread a thin layer of spaghetti sauce. Arrange a layer of lasagne noodles, placed lengthwise over sauce. Spread one third of the remaining sauce over noodles, then a second layer of lasagne noodles placed width-wise.
- Cover with all the cottage cheese mixture and half the mozzarella cheese slices then another third of the spaghetti sauce.
- Place the final layer of lasagne noodles lengthwise, cover with remainder of the spaghetti sauce and the rest of the mozzarella cheese slices.
- Sprinkle with parmesan cheese.
- Bake at 350°F (180°C) for 40 minutes. Let stand for 10 minutes before serving.

Serves 8.

Per Serving:
Protein . . . . .35 g
Fat . . . . .18 g
Carbohydrates . . . . .70 g
Calories 593
Dietary Fiber . . . . .10 g

Fettucine with Vegetables

Beans and pasta discover each other. The result – a main dish that will aid an out-of-whack entertaining budget. Imagine pasta primavera with a crunch!

1 lb	fettucine	450 g
2 tsp	olive oil	10 mL
1	large red pepper, cut in 1½" (3.5 cm) strips	1
1	clove garlic, minced	1
1	zucchini, cut in 1½" (3.5 cm) strips	1
3	green onions, chopped	3
2 Tbsp	butter or margarine	25 mL
2 tsp	lemon juice	10 mL
½ tsp	grated lemon rind	3 mL
2 tsp	Dijon mustard	10 mL
⅓ cup	chicken stock*	75 mL
1½ cups	canned chick peas, drained and rinsed	375 mL
3 Tbsp	fresh parsley, chopped	45 mL
½ tsp	dried basil	3 mL
	salt and pepper to taste	

* Can use bouillon cubes or instant granules. Follow package instructions.

- In skillet, sauté red pepper and garlic in oil over medium heat for 3 minutes. Add zucchini and green onions and cook 2 minutes more. Remove vegetables from pan.
- Melt butter in skillet. Add lemon juice, rind, mustard and stock. Stir.
- Add vegetables, chick peas, basil and parsley. Heat for 5 minutes.
- While making sauce, cook fettucine in boiling water until tender, following package directions. Drain.
- Add sauce to fettucine. Toss and heat through.
- Serve on warmed plates. Sprinkle with freshly grated parmesan cheese.

Per Serving:	
Protein	22 g
Fat	8 g
Carbohydrates	108 g
Calories	593
Dietary Fiber	8 g

Serves 4.

Yellow Split Pea Dahl

Dahl is a traditional Indian dish and this is one of the many variations. It is a prime source of protein in India. Use leftovers for wraps using roti instead of tortillas.

1 Tbsp	vegetable oil	15 mL
1	medium onion, chopped	1
2	cloves garlic, minced	2
2	medium carrots, chopped	2
3/4 cup	dried yellow split peas	175 mL
1 1/2 cups	chicken stock*	375 mL
1 tsp	turmeric	5 mL
1 tsp	chili powder	5 mL
1 1/2 tsp	ground ginger	8 mL
1 tsp	coriander	3 mL
1	medium zucchini, cut in 1/2" (1 cm) cubes	1
1 cup	canned crushed tomatoes	250 mL
2 cups	hot cooked brown rice	500 ml
1 1/2 cups	hot cooked broccoli (optional)	375 mL

Can use chicken bouillon cube or instant granules.

- In a large saucepan, sauté onion, garlic and carrots in oil over medium heat until tender, about 5 minutes.
- Add split peas, stock & spices. Reduce heat, cover and simmer 45 minutes.
- Add zucchini and tomatoes and simmer for another 20 minutes, stirring occasionally.
- On individual serving plates, mound rice. Place broccoli on the rice and spoon dahl mixture over both. Serve with yogurt and chopped cilantro if desired.

Serves 4.

Per Serving:
Protein . . . . .15 g
Fat . . . . 5 g
Carbohydrates . . . . .63 g
Calories 348
Dietary Fiber . . . . 8 g

Red Lentil Dahl

Here is another East Indian-inspired variation of a dahl which is quick to make and tasty. This dahl makes a good filling for wraps – use rotis instead of tortillas for a more authentic meal.

1 cup	red lentils	250 mL
3 cups	water	750 mL
1/2 tsp	turmeric	3 mL
1 Tbsp	olive oil	15 mL
1	medium onion, chopped	1
1	clove garlic, minced	1
1	can (71/2 oz/196 mL) tomato paste	1
1 cup	water	250 mL
2 tsp	garam masala*	10 mL
1/2 tsp	salt	3 mL

* Garam masala is a south asian spice which you may have to look for at a speciality store. If unavailable, use 2 tsp (10 mL) curry powder and 1 tsp (5 mL) of coriander.

- Add lentils and turmeric to water and simmer for 15 minutes. Drain.
- While lentils are cooking, sauté onion and garlic in oil over medium heat for 5 minutes.
- Add onion mixture, tomato paste, water, garam masala and salt to lentils. Simmer for 15-20 minutes.
- Serve over rice.

Serves 4.

Garam marsala is a blend of coriander, cumin, cinnamon and cardamon.

Per Serving:
Protein . . . . 6 g
Fat . . . . 4 g
Carbohydrates . . . . .22 g
Calories 137
Dietary Fiber . . . . 5 g

Chick Pea Curry

The friend who gave us this recipe said, "You can curry almost anything". She did as she stretched her budget to feed her family of eight. Here is a vegetarian adaptation made with chick peas. It is important to use a good quality Indian curry powder.

2 Tbsp	vegetable oil	25 mL
1	large onion, finely chopped	1
1 Tbsp	curry powder (more if desired)	15 mL
2 Tbsp	flour	25 mL
2 cups	vegetable or chicken stock *	500 mL
1/2 cup	raisins	125 mL
1/4 cup	coconut**	50 mL
1	apple, peeled and grated	1
1 tsp	tomato ketchup	5 mL
1 tsp	sugar	5 mL
1 tsp	Worcestershire sauce	5 mL
1	can (19 oz/540 mL) chick peas, drained & rinsed	1
1 1/2 cups	cooked rice (long grain converted is nice)	375 mL

Can use bouillon cubes or instant granules. Follow package instructions.
*** You can use 1/4 cup (50 mL) coconut milk instead.*

- In deep skillet, sauté onion in oil over medium heat until tender, about 5 minutes. Stir in curry powder and flour.
- Add stock slowly, stirring constantly.
- Add all other ingredients except chick peas and rice. Simmer for 15-20 minutes. Adjust seasoning.
- Add chick peas and heat through, about 5 minutes.
- Serve over cooked rice. Chutney is a great accompaniment.

Serves 4.

```
Per Serving:
Protein ..................14 g
Fat .....................12 g
Carbohydrates ..........82 g
Calories ................479
Dietary Fiber ...........10 g
```

Spicy Vegetable Medley

This tempting mix of vegetables and chick peas makes a delicious side dish or a full meal over rice.

2 Tbsp	vegetable oil	25 mL
1	medium onion, chopped	1
1	clove garlic, mined	1
1 Tbsp	curry powder	15 mL
1 tsp	ground cumin	5 mL
1/4 tsp	ground allspice	2 mL
1 tsp	ground ginger	5 mL
1	can (4 oz/114 mL) diced green chilies	1
1 Tbsp	flour*	15 mL
2 cups	vegetable or chicken stock**	500 mL
2	medium carrots, chopped	2
2	medium potatoes, chopped	2
1/2	small cauliflower, chopped	1/2
1 cup	green beans, cut in 1" (2.5 cm) slices	250 mL
1	medium apple, peeled and chopped	1
1	can (19 oz/540 mL) chick peas, drained & rinsed	1

If serving as a side dish, use 1 cup (250 mL) stock and 1 1/2 tsp (8 mL) flour.
*** Can use bouillon cubes or instant granules. Follow package directions.*

- In skillet, sauté onion in oil over medium heat for 5 minutes. Add garlic, curry powder, spices and green chilies. Stir for 2 minutes more.
- Add flour and blend for 1 minute. Gradually stir in stock. Continue to stir until mixture boils and thickens slightly.
- Add vegetables. Cover and simmer for about 10 minutes until vegetables are tender.
- Add apples and chick peas and heat through.
- Serve over cooked brown rice or your favorite pasta.

Serves 6.

Per Serving:
Protein . . . . 9 g
Fat . . . . 6 g
Carbohydrates . . . . .38 g
Calories 235
Dietary Fiber . . . . 7 g

Gratin of White Beans with Herbs

Served with a tossed salad and crusty bread, this makes a satisfying meal. Also can be a side dish with lamb or pork. This recipe makes an large amount so it can easily be halved.

2½ cups	dried navy or Great Northern beans	625 mL
3 Tbsp	olive oil	45 mL
1	medium onion, chopped	1
2	cloves garlic, minced	2
2	fresh tomatoes, peeled and chopped	2
½ cup	chicken stock*	125 mL
½ cup	whipping cream (half and half works)	125 mL
	salt and pepper to taste	
Topping:		
1½ cups	bread crumbs	375 mL
2	green onions, finely chopped	2
⅓ cup	butter or margarine, melted	75 mL
2 tsp	each, dried rosemary, thyme**	10 mL
⅓ cup	fresh parsley, chopped	75 mL

Can use chicken bouillon cubes or instant granules. Follow package directions.
**Use fresh if available, but remember to use 3 times as much.*

- Soak beans using quick-soak method on page 15. Drain and rinse.
- In large saucepan, cover beans with water. Cover and cook over low heat until tender, about 45 minutes. Drain and rinse.
- In skillet sauté onion and garlic in oil over medium heat for 5 minutes. Add tomatoes and cook 10 minutes more, stirring frequently.
- Add stock, cream, salt and pepper and stir another 2 minutes.
- In large lightly oiled casserole, place beans and stir in other ingredients.
- Mix topping ingredients together and sprinkle on bean mixture. Bake at 375°F (190°C), uncovered, for 30 minutes.

Serves 8.

Per Serving:
Protein . . . . .17 g
Fat . . . . .19 g
Carbohydrates . . . . .57 g
Calories 459
Dietary Fiber . . . . .25 g

Vegetables & Side Dishes

Broccoli & Chick Peas

The nutty flavor of chick peas, combined with broccoli, makes a novel pairing. Many people don't realize that you only need to cut the bottom inch off the broccoli stalk. Peel the rest of the stem – it's all usable.

1 Tbsp	vegetable oil	15 mL
5	medium stalks broccoli, stems peeled and sliced, heads cut into small florets	5
3 Tbsp	water	45 mL
1	can (19 oz/540 mL) chick peas (garbanzo beans), drained and rinsed	1
½ cup	canned artichoke hearts, chopped	125 mL
2 Tbsp	oil from artichokes	25 mL
2 tsp	fine herbs	10 mL
4-6	sun dried tomatoes, cut in strips (optional)	4-6

- In skillet or wok, heat oil over medium heat. Add broccoli and stir-fry for 3-5 minutes.
- Add water and cover. Cook for about 3 minutes (broccoli should still be a little crunchy).
- Add other ingredients and heat through.

Serves 6.

An effective way to add fiber to the diet while cutting fat is to substitute plant sources of protein such as legumes for animal sources like meats.

Per Serving:
Protein .... 8 g
Fat .... 8 g
Carbohydrates ....24 g
Calories 194
Dietary Fiber .... 6 g

Zucchini Garbanzo Stir-fry

This side dish is excellent served with cold ham or chicken. Most economical when your friends start presenting you with their excess produce in September.

1	red onion, sliced in rings	1
2	small zucchinis, cut in 1/4" (0.5 cm) slices	2
1 Tbsp	vegetable oil	15 mL
1	large fresh tomato, chopped	1
1 cup	canned garbanzo beans (chick peas), drained and rinsed	250 mL
1 tsp	dried thyme	5 mL
1 tsp	dried basil	5 mL
	salt and pepper to taste	

- In skillet, sauté onion and zucchini in oil over medium heat for 3 minutes.
- Stir in tomatoes, garbanzo beans, basil and thyme.
- Cover and simmer 15 minutes or until zucchini is tender.
- Taste and adjust seasonings.

Serves 4.

```
Per Serving:
Protein .................. 6 g
Fat ..................... 5 g
Carbohydrates ..........19 g
Calories ................139
Dietary Fiber ............ 5 g
```

Bean Counter's Medley

Accountants would give the nod to investing in this vegetable dish for company. The bottom line is lots of value for your money, and the extra dividend – delicious!

1	can (14 oz/398 mL) crushed tomatoes	1
1/4 cup	vinegar	50 mL
1/2 cup	tomato ketchup	125 mL
1 cup	celery, chopped	250 mL
1	large onion, cut in rings	1
1	can (19 oz/540 mL) kidney beans	1
1	can (19 oz/540 mL) lima beans	1
1	can (14 oz/398 mL) cut green beans*	1
1	can (14 oz/398 mL) cut yellow beans	1
1	can (14 oz/398 mL) baked beans, undrained	1

Can use 10 oz (300 g) package of frozen green beans.

- In large casserole, combine crushed tomatoes, vinegar and ketchup.
- Add onions, green pepper and celery.
- Drain liquid from all the beans except baked beans. Add all beans to the casserole mixture. Stir well
- Bake, covered in 350°F (180°C) oven for 45 minutes.

Serves 8-10.

Per Serving:
Protein . . . . .10 g
Fat . . . . 1 g
Carbohydrates . . . . .42 g
Calories 199
Dietary Fiber . . . . .12 g

Stuffed Baked Potatoes

You only need 1/4 cup (50 mL) of black beans for this recipe so hopefully you have frozen, cooked beans tucked away. For a light supper, a green salad is all that is needed. Add either baked chicken or a broiled steak if hunger demands.

4	medium baking potatoes, scrubbed	4
3	stalks broccoli	3
1 Tbsp	olive oil	15 mL
1/2	red pepper, chopped	1/2
1	small zucchini, cut in quarters lengthwise and sliced	1
8	medium mushrooms, sliced	8
1 tsp	ground cumin	5 mL
1 Tbsp	butter or margarine	15 mL
2 Tbsp	plain yogurt	25 mL
1/4 cup	cooked black beans	50 mL
1/3 cup	cheddar or Monterey Jack cheese, shredded	75 mL

- Bake potatoes for 1 hour at 400°F (200°C) or until tender.
- While potatoes are baking, wash and peel broccoli stems and slice. Cut florets into small pieces.
- In skillet, heat oil over medium heat. Sauté broccoli and red peppers for 5 minutes
- Add zucchini and mushrooms. Sauté about 5 minutes more or until vegetables are tender.
- When potatoes are done, cut in half lengthwise. Remove the insides leaving 1/4" (0.5 cm) on the skin. Put the rest in a bowl. Mash and add butter, yogurt, cumin, beans and vegetables.
- Place potato cases in a 13" x 9" (22cm x 33 cm) baking pan. Spoon vegetable mixture into potato cases. Top with cheese.
- Bake for 10 minutes at 350°F (180°C) until cheese melts.

Serves 4 generously.

```
Per Serving:
Protein . . . . . . . . . . . . . . . . .11 g
Fat . . . . . . . . . . . . . . . . . . . . .10 g
Carbohydrates . . . . . . . . . .37 g
Calories . . . . . . . . . . . . . . . .268
Dietary Fiber . . . . . . . . . . .7 g
```

Tomato Lima Bean Parmigiana

Our recipe card for this one is dog-eared and spotted. Serve with ham and a baked potato for maximum oven use. Can also be used as a main dish if you double the amount of bacon.

4	strips bacon, cut in ½" (1 cm) slices	4
1	onion, chopped finely	1
1	can (14 oz/398 mL) lima beans, drained and rinsed*	1
2	cloves garlic, minced	2
1 cup	water	250 mL
2	medium tomatoes, chopped	2
½ cup	grated parmesan cheese	125 mL

- In skillet, cook bacon over medium heat until crisp. Remove from pan and pat with paper towel to remove excess fat.
- In ovenproof casserole, combine all ingredients except cheese.
- Sprinkle cheese on top. Bake, uncovered, at 325°F (160°C) for 25 minutes or until bubbly

Serves 4.

Use the above recipe or any bean and rice mixture to stuff green or red peppers. Slice pepper vertically for a different look.

Per Serving:
Protein . . . . .13 g
Fat . . . . 8 g
Carbohydrates . . . . .19 g
Calories 194
Dietary Fiber . . . . 4 g

Curried Cauliflower with Beans

Tired of cauliflower with cheese sauce? This is an unlikely combination of flavors and colors, but it works!

1/2 tsp	ground ginger	3 mL
2	cloves garlic, minced	2
1 Tbsp	vegetable oil	15 mL
1	cauliflower, cut in florets	1
2	tomatoes, finely chopped	2
2 Tbsp	lime juice	25 mL
1 tsp	curry powder	5 mL
3 Tbsp	water	45 mL
1 cup	red kidney beans, drained and rinsed	250 mL

- In a medium saucepan, sauté garlic and ginger in oil over medium heat for 2 minutes.
- Stir in tomatoes, lime juice, curry powder and water. Simmer for 3 minutes.
- Add cauliflower, cover and simmer over medium heat for 8 minutes.
- Add beans. Stir and heat thoroughly.
- Taste and adjust seasonings.

Serves 4-6.

Per Serving:	
Protein	8 g
Fat	4 g
Carbohydrates	22 g
Calories	145
Dietary Fiber	8 g

White Beans Provence

This recipe is an attempt to come close to a delicious bean dish served with lamb shanks in a Napa Valley restaurant. It's hard to dissect a dish under the critical eye of the waiter, but this one was worth the effort. Excellent as a side dish for any meat.

1 Tbsp	olive oil	15 mL
1	medium onion, chopped	1
1/2 cup	celery, finely chopped	125 mL
2	medium tomatoes, finely chopped	2
2 cups	cooked white beans*	500 mL
1 cup	chicken stock**	250 mL
1 tsp	dried thyme	5 mL
2 Tbsp	fresh parsley, finely chopped	25 mL
	salt and pepper to taste	

*Soak and cook 1 cup (250 mL) dried according to directions on page 15 and 16.
** Can use chicken bouillon or instant granules. Follow package directions.

- In saucepan, sauté onion and celery in oil over medium heat for 5 minutes.
- Add rest of ingredients except parsley. Simmer, covered, for 20 minutes, stirring occasionally.
- Add parsley and salt and pepper. Cook 5 minutes more.

Serves 6.

Per Serving:
Protein . . . . 6 g
Fat . . . . 3 g
Carbohydrates . . . . .19 g
Calories 119
Dietary Fiber . . . . 7 g

Refried Beans

A bean book wouldn't be complete without a recipe for refried beans. They are served as a side dish with many Mexican meals but can also be used as a filling for burritos or spread on tortillas.

1 cup	dried pinto or red beans*	250 mL
1	bay leaf	1
1	dried red chili	1
3 Tbsp	vegetable oil or bacon fat	45 mL
1	medium onion, chopped	1
2	cloves garlic, minced	2
1	tomato, peeled and chopped finely	1
1¹/₂ tsp	ground cumin	8 mL
¹/₂ tsp	salt	2 mL
	freshly ground pepper	

Can use 14 oz/398 mL can of beans. Do not drain. Add dried red chili and omit steps one and two.

- Soak beans using quick-soak method, page 15.
- In large saucepan, place beans, bay leaf, red chili in 1 inch (2.5 cm) of water. Bring to boil, cover and simmer for 35-45 minutes until beans are soft. Check during cooking to be sure the beans are not dry. If necessary, add a little more water. Do not drain.
- Remove bay leaf.
- Purée undrained beans in food process or blender.
- While beans are cooking, in skillet, sauté onion and garlic in oil over medium heat for 5 minutes. Add tomato, cumin, salt and pepper and cook for 5 minutes more.
- Add puréed beans, a little at a time, to onion mixture, stirring after each addition. Add a little more oil if necessary to give a thick creamy paste.

Yields 2 cups (500 mL).

```
Per Serving:
Protein . . . . . . . . . . . . . . . . .11 g
Fat . . . . . . . . . . . . . . . . . . . . .11 g
Carbohydrates . . . . . . . . . .34 g
Calories . . . . . . . . . . . . . . . .271
Dietary Fiber . . . . . . . . . . . .20 g
```

Black Beans & Rice

Perk up white rice with the addition of beans. The vinegar gives it an extra tang.

1	can (14 oz/398 mL) black beans, drained and rinsed, or 1³/₄ cups cooked*	1
1 Tbsp	vegetable oil	15 mL
2	cloves garlic, minced	2
¹/₂	green pepper, chopped	¹/₂
¹/₂ tsp	dried oregano	3 mL
3 Tbsp	white vinegar	45 mL
1¹/₂ cups	rice	375 mL

If using dried beans, prepare ³/₄ cup (175 mL) according to soaking and cooking instructions on pages 15 and 16.

- Cook rice according to package directions.
- In skillet, sauté pepper and garlic in oil over medium heat for 3 minutes or until just soft.
- Turn off heat and stir beans, oregano and vinegar into skillet mixture.
- When rice is ready, add bean mixture to it. Heat through

Serves 6.

Per Serving:	
Protein	*9 g*
Fat	*3 g*
Carbohydrates	*53 g*
Calories	*276*
Dietary Fiber	*4 g*

Caribbean Rice

This is an adaptation of a traditional Caribbean dish. A treat for lovers of spicy food. Mates well with grilled white fish.

1¼ cups	dried black-eyed peas	300 mL
2 tsp	vegetable oil	10 mL
1	small red pepper, chopped	1
1	medium onion, chopped	1
3	cloves garlic, minced	3
3	ripe tomatoes, chopped	3
½ cup	uncooked white rice (preferably converted)	125 mL
1 cup	vegetable or chicken stock*	250 mL
½ cup	pitted black olives, chopped	125 mL
½ tsp	ground allspice	3 mL
½ tsp	freshly ground pepper	3 mL
¼ tsp	cayenne pepper	1 mL
	salt to taste	
2	green onions, chopped (optional)	2

Can use bouillon cubes or instant granules. Follow package instructions.

- Cook black-eyed peas in 3 cups (750 mL) water for 25-30 minutes. Drain.
- In deep skillet, sauté red pepper, onion and garlic in oil over medium heat for 5 minutes.
- Add tomatoes and rice, stir for 1 minute.
- Add remaining ingredients, except green onions, and simmer covered until rice is cooked, about 20 minutes. Add a little more stock if mixture gets too dry.
- Add green onions and stir gently.

Serves 6.

Per Serving:
Protein . . . . 4 g
Fat . . . . 6 g
Carbohydrates . . . . .26 g
Calories 171
Dietary Fiber . . . . 4 g

Jamaican Peas & Rice

Serve this with your favorite chicken dish. Goes well with jerk chicken. In Jamaica, "peas" are actually red kidney beans.

1 cup	chopped onion	250 mL
1/2 cup	chopped red or green pepper	125 mL
3	cloves, garlic, minced	3
1/2-1	Scotch bonnet or Habanero pepper	1/2-1
1 1/2 tsp	dried thyme leaves	8 mL
1/2 tsp	ground allspice	3 mL
1 Tbsp	oil	15 mL
1	14 oz/398 mL chicken broth or 1 can (14oz/398 mL) light coconut milk	1
2	cans (14oz/398mL) red kidney beans, drained and rinsed	2
2 cups	peeled sweet potatoes, cubed	500mL
1/4 cup	lime juice	50 mL
2 cups	cooked rice	500 mL

- Saute onion, pepper, garlic, Scotch bonnet pepper, thyme and allspice in oil in a medium saucepan for 3-4 minutes.
- Add chicken broth or coconut milk, beans and sweet potatoes. Heat to boiling. Reduce heat and simmer, uncovered, until potatoes are tender, about 10-15 minutes. Stir in lime juice.
- Serve over rice. Serve with your favorite chicken dish (it goes well with jerk chicken).

Serves 4-6.

```
Per Serving:
Protein . . . . . . . . . . . . . . . . . 12 g
Fat . . . . . . . . . . . . . . . . . . . . . 4 g
Carbohydrates . . . . . . . . . . 53 g
Calories . . . . . . . . . . . . . . . . 289
Dietary Fiber . . . . . . . . . . . 15 g
```

Red Beans & Rice

A very popular New Orleans dish. Too nourishing not to be enjoyed everywhere.

1 cup	cooked kidney beans or small red Mexican beans*	250 mL
3/4 cup	brown rice	175 mL
2 tsp	vegetable oil	10 mL
1	onion, chopped	1
2	cloves garlic, minced	2
1/2	green pepper, chopped	1/2
1	can (14 oz/398 mL) diced tomatoes	1
1	bay leaf	1
1 tsp	dried basil	5 mL
4	drops hot pepper sauce (e.g. Tabasco)	4
	salt and pepper to taste	

If using dried beans, prepare 1/2 cup (125 mL) according to soaking and cooking instructions on pages 15 and 16.

- Cook brown rice according to package directions.
- In skillet, sauté onion, garlic and green pepper in oil over medium heat for 5 minutes.
- Add beans, tomatoes and rest of the ingredients, except rice. Simmer for 15 minutes. Remove bay leaf.
- Place cooked rice in warm bowls. Pour bean mixture over rice.

Serves 4-6.

Per Serving:
Protein . . . . 8 g
Fat . . . . 4 g
Carbohydrates . . . . .46 g
Calories 241
Dietary Fiber . . . . 7 g

Index

About the Author

Before turning her attention to bean cuisine, Trish Ross had a successful career as a special education teacher and adult educator. For the past 10 years, Ross has been extensively researching the world of beans. With this new edition of Easy Beans, Ross has made bean cookery a delicious and healthy choice for today's busy cooks. She lives in Vancouver, B.C.

Order Form

Please send me:

____ copies of **Easy Beans** (revised edition) X $16.95 Cdn or $12.95 US/ book = _____

____ copies of **More Easy Beans** X $16.95 Cdn or $12.95 US/ book = _____
(taxes included)

Plus Shipping & Handling ($3 for first book, $2 for each additional book) = _____

TOTAL ENCLOSED: _____

SPECIAL OFFER:
Buy both books for $25 Cdn or $20 US plus $5 shipping and handling

NAME: _____

STREET _____

CITY _____ PROV/STATE _____

POSTAL/ZIP CODE _____ PHONE _____

Please make the cheque or money order payable to: Big Bean Publishing and mail to:
Big Bean Publishing, #201 - 1508 Mariners Walk
Vancouver, BC Canada V6J 4X9